Beyond Revival
Living in the Spirit of Revolution

by John L. Mastrogiovanni, D.Min.

Published by
Morris Publishing
Additional copies available.
See segment, "For Additional Copies of this Book and Other Material."

Copyright © 1999
John L. Mastrogiovanni, D.Min.
ISBN: 0-7392-0191-3
Library of Congress Catalog Card Number: 99-93209

All rights reserved. No part of this book may be reproduced in any form without written permission from the author, except for brief quotations in a review.

FOR ADDITIONAL COPIES OF
THIS BOOK AND OTHER MATERIAL

Additional copies of this book may be obtained by contacting:

Mastrogiovanni Ministries
c/o Jesus Is Lord Christian Center
P.O. Box 1522
Monrovia, CA 91017
(626) 357-6797

In addition, we recommend Dr. Mastrogiovanni's book:
THE SPIRIT OF THE SCORPION
"Conquering the Powers of Insurrection"

"My brother in Christ has not only pinpointed one of the greatest problems in the Church, but also offers a sound, logical and biblical solution. I make this a 'Must Read Book' for all my leaders and would suggest the same for all Churches!"

Rev. Robert J. (Bob) Spurgeon, M.Div.
Senior Pastor, First Christian Church

Dr. Mastrogiovanni is available for speaking engagements. Please call or write the ministry office.

Printed in the USA by

MP
MORRIS PUBLISHING

3212 East Highway 30 • Kearney, NE 68847 • 1-800-650-7888

TABLE OF CONTENTS

FORWARD
By Bishop James O'Neal, B.S. M.B.A., Ph.D., D.Div.

REVIVAL

CHAPTER ONE
Revival – Part of a Process

CHAPTER TWO
Revival – The Change

CHAPTER THREE
Revival – The Grindstone

CHAPTER FOUR
Revival – The Awakening

CHAPTER FIVE
Revival – The Refreshing

REVOLUTION

CHAPTER SIX
Revolution – The Burning

CHAPTER SEVEN
Revolution – The Transformation

CHAPTER EIGHT
Revolution – Facing a New Tomorrow

CHAPTER NINE
Revolution - Abortion and Rebirth

CHAPTER TEN
Revolution – Transcendent Love

Forward

As a minister called to minister to other ministers and the church at large, this book brings clear focus and revelation to the passion of most leaders who ask me to speak for their church revivals.

Dr. John Mastrogiovanni takes the painstaking effort to change the ancient denominational paradigm of, "Let's have a revival," and provides an appropriate shift to, "Let's start a revolution in our city."

This is a powerful book that will bring the reader to a new level of evangelism that will change forever the climate and spirit of their church, city and even the world.

by Bishop James M. O'Neal, B.S. M.B.A., Ph.D, D.Div

Chapter One
Revival – Part of a Process

"Revival" - A word so often used in the Christian church to depict spiritual awakening, the blossoming of excitement over the notion of serving God, and a resurgence of an evangelical thrust in which lost souls are saved and filled. *"Revival"* - A word used to depict the outpouring of God's presence on the local church or the church at large. A word used to describe the inner change of a person's life from a lethargic expression of worship, to a sincere passion for fellowship with God. *"Revival"* - A word used to depict the revitalization of that which was once...alive.

Over the years, our congregation, like multitudes of others, has cried out to God for the waters of revival. Yet, in recent years (especially the past twenty-five), revival is not occurring in the manner as we have heard and read about previously. To put it plainly, many churches and ministries have had or are experiencing pockets of revival, some lasting for weeks, others for several years. But few of them beyond that, where nations and cities are completely changed. We know the potential for changing cities and nations is possible, and many of the pockets of revival that are now occurring have the "potential" to do just that. But the one thing history has proven to us is that ***revival in itself is fleeting.*** If God intended revival to be the key to saving the world, then we would not be here, the Reformation would have brought the conclusion of the age and we would all be glorified before the throne of the Lord. Let us then pose the obvious but frightening questions, "Why if we have experienced revival in the past (either personally or corporately) does God seemingly need to send revival after revival?" "Why must He reopen the flood gates of

His presence, after He promised that He would never leave us or forsake us?" The bottom-line question is: *"Why do the waters of revival seem to dry out?"*

While there may be many contributing factors and theological essays, I believe one reason stands out above them all. Many times the answer I am about to share with you is overlooked in light of all the others. In actuality, I believe that the other answers would not even exist if we would embrace this one. After all, from talking with some ministers and theologians, Christians cannot resolve that the revival experience is needed in the traditional sense anyway. For example, some have said, "Why must God do something special, if the Spirit of God is already dwelling in us?" Or, "If He is dwelling in us, than why do we even need more?" On the other hand, some philosophize that revival is the high point of church life, but hindered due to sin in the lives of believers. Others point out that the scriptures state it is because of our sinful condition that God reaches out and sends revival. So why do we struggle toward revival over and over? Why has the downpour of most former revivals dried out? The answer is simply that revival is intended for "something greater." **Revival is only part of a process** and that process is called, **"spiritual revolution."**

Most of the biblical examples we have of what is termed, *"revival,"* in fact, move into something far greater than what we have embraced. For example, Jesus, our Lord, clearly had the earmark of a revivalist, but to Him revival was only part of that something greater...*spiritual revolution.* If revival was what we termed earlier, the Savior did all that. He brought spiritual reawakening to God's people. He energized excitement where His followers reached out to others. He brought the waters of God's presence back to dry and oppressed believers. He took the lives of people who were lethargic in worship and drew them into a passion to fellowship with His Father. But where most of us falter is when He took the next step.

On that wonderful day we call Palm Sunday, He took what was then a powerful revival (where multitudes heralded praise), and moved into *spiritual revolution*. It was during that time His "followship" dropped off; multitudes were then nowhere to be found and the excitement of *"the now revival"* was weighed down with **the responsibility of the future.** This is where most of us in the church-world falter. It is here where we begin to cry out again for another revival (thinking that in some way we have missed it or that God has stopped doing what we thought was His Will), **when in reality, while *WE* were still putting the finishing touches to our revival tent (or shrine), God left the revival "briefing" and went to the battle-lines of spiritual revolution.** An example of this is Gideon, a revivalist/revolutionist, who brought a refreshing revival to the people of God who were oppressed by the Midianites. Multitudes followed him, but when it came time to move into spiritual revolution, his numbers were reduced to a handful of people. It was through this *spirit of revolution* that he and his small band of revolutionaries brought radical change during his lifetime.

Revival is intended to birth a *spiritual revolution.* It is a means to an end, not an end from the means of prayer, repentance and spiritual discipline. It is not something we can plan on our church calendars and say that Brother or Sister so-and-so is coming to our church for a week of "revival meetings." Revival is not the product of prayer, repentance and spiritual discipline, but rather prayer, repentance and spiritual discipline is part of *true* revival. When a believer or a church has a desire for prayer, repentance and deeper fellowship with God, this is a sign that the waters of revival are already beginning to flow and the first side of a two-sided coin. An awakening has happened. People are beginning to discover who they are and to what they are called. Then, when the other aspects of revival come (like the other side of the coin), the excitement of worship, the desire for evangelism, the inner stirrings of transformed lives, and new believers coming into the church, we need to stop and ask, "God, how can we cash this coin in for spiritual revolution?! How can we change the face of our land, our city, and our nation?" God will respond by leading us into spiritual revolution, not necessarily a formula or a program, *but massive change.*

We know that this can be encountered, because the scripture is full of imperfect people who were revivalists, turned revolutionists. We know it can be experienced in *our lifetime,* because many of the denominations and ministries that exist today are the products of one or two people who, in their lifetime, went *beyond revival into spiritual revolution.* The problem is when the waters of revival and the fires of revolution are only limited to a few revolutionaries. In spite of this however, results have been astounding. Many church buildings that exist today have the names of such past denominational and non-denominational movements of God. But like in the days of Jesus, the people in the *revival* would have more readily made Jesus their king right then (John 6:15), rather than going with Him into the fires of *revolution.* Many denominational and non-denominational churches are crowded with people, **securing themselves *unknowingly* to the shrine** of a former spiritual revolutionary or a former revolutionary theology, **rather than becoming, experiencing and expressing** what those early revolutionaries did to change the course of history.

* * * * * *

The following pages of this book are intended for the reader to take a biblical journey through scripture and discover the process of revival and revolution. Can you imagine what it would be like if the next spiritual revolution was not limited to a handful of people? Can you imagine what it would be like if the Body of Christ (the Church at large) discovered what it was destined to be...the agent of spiritual revolution? Can you imagine if the majority of us in the church (local and at large), all moved forward toward that spiritual revolution? *Not only can we imagine it, but*

God is actively moving us toward that end. If we would open our hearts to spiritual revolution, not only would revival come, but by the time you turned the page of this book, we would all be before the throne of the King of the Universe, the Lord Jesus Christ, in glorious splendor.

Chapter Two
Revival – The Change

The Christian (the only created being on the face of this planet who has a living future beyond this world, a genuine purpose in this world, and a given destiny to change this world), for some reason struggles with the oppression of a forgotten identity and the despair of a lost sense of destiny. How can this be? After all, most believers have a ready answer for their destiny, saying that heaven is their future and that their identity is in the person of Jesus Christ. But if that belief truly impassions us, then why do we go through our every day life with moments of blessing followed by long periods of an awareness of dissatisfaction? Why is it that our Christian stability depends on and spends most of its time, trying to minimize our slavery to the quiet sadness of discontentment? In reality, we live life trying to cope with the heaviness of oppression rather than breaking free from it and leaving it far behind. Please keep in mind, I am not saying that if you were to ask the average believer wrestling with such feelings, "Do you want to break free?" they would say, "No," but that the proof of our need and our congregational condition is in the type of services and ministry focus we have. Sure, every church worth its pastor's weight in gold would say, "We have a vision to reach the world and make disciples for Christ." Yet, it seems that we are like the children of Israel in the days of young Moses. They would have wonderful times of worship as long as it was socially acceptable. They had mediocre careers (slavery) in Pharaoh's pyramid building project. They would protest against injustice as long it didn't cost them their livelihood and those who were radical when it did, were either considered extremists or martyrs. Thus, the children of Israel though inherently mighty, lived by moments of blessing and long periods of oppression.

> *Exod 1:7-14* 7 But the children of Israel were fruitful and increased abundantly, multiplied and grew exceedingly mighty; and the land was filled with them. 8 Now there arose a new king over Egypt, who did not know Joseph. 9 And he said to his people, "Look, the people of the children of Israel are more and mightier than we; 10 "come, let us deal shrewdly with them, lest they multiply, and it happen, in the event of war, that they also join our enemies and fight against us, and so go up out of the land." 11 Therefore they set taskmasters over them to afflict them with their burdens. And they built for Pharaoh supply cities, Pithom and Raamses. 12 But the more they afflicted them, the more they multiplied and grew. And they were in dread of the children of Israel. 13 So the Egyptians made the children of Israel serve with rigor. 14 And they made their lives bitter with hard bondage-- in mortar, in brick, and in all manner of service in the field. All their service in which they made them serve was with rigor. (NKJ)

The children of Israel were not children of the world, but the children of God. They were people of covenant and had a calling to destiny. Don't be confused by theological prejudice. The scripture is not talking about the lost in this passage; it is talking about God's people. The children of Israel lived their life on the basis of past blessings rather than their future purpose. The scripture said that they were fruitful and they increased; they were mighty and the land was filled with them. (Sounds like a blessed church to me.) But when a new Pharaoh came on the scene, times changed, but God's people didn't. Rather than letting go of a past success, and moving to the next phase of destiny, they held on. The result was affliction and heavy burdens. Stop for a moment and think of the average Christian who attends church and has done so for at least three years. How many of them (us) are suddenly challenged with a resurgence of worldly affections or a lethargic complacency? It is here where the "cruise-a-matic" is born. All of a sudden there is discontentment. We even begin to pray, but rather than press into what God has prepared, the overwhelming nervousness (created by the need of discontentment), moves us to a spiritual *"fast food"* take-out line, rather than letting God cook us one of His perfect homemade meals. Many times we make what seems to be a spiritual, even graceful exit from the congregation where we attend. In this condition, we inherently know we need change, but a pattern sets in. Seeking for a new congregation to stimulate us into a new (usually called "deeper") experience with God, **we actually seek an external experience rather than the internal working of our Creator.** We don't realize it, but we are seeking the stimulation that the past blessing (or revival) brought us. *(If we happen to be a leader in the church or even the pastor, many times this is when "we" start "planning" revival meetings, rather than "manifesting" them.)* This lasts for a while, but as soon as we begin to look to God with some real honesty, we find the discontentment all over again. In some cases we may join a particular facet of church ministry knowing that we need to "be involved". But in the end, it is the same story, "Pastor, I feel that God is leading me to another church. I feel like my days here are coming to an end; I am resigning from my position. Please understand, it has nothing to do with you or the church; God is just leading me elsewhere." What we don't understand is that subtle erosion is taking place. It is intended for positive results, but many times our resistance to the process causes it to turn for the worst. It is about who we are, the destiny of our lives and our connection to the eternal Kingdom. It's about God attempting to bring us to a point of true revival, to birth in us *the spirit of revolution.* But rather than discover a brokenness to build our future, our reaction opens the door to the cunning, gradual enslaving of darkness. In reality, Satan recognizes our purpose and destiny, and he is doing all he can to keep us from identifying it. It means that he has recognized (as Pharaoh did), that the people of God are mighty and in a direct confrontation, a conflict would be devastating for him. So like a puppy tied to a tree in the backyard, he gets us going in circles through what appears to be "meaningful," maybe even "exciting" stimulation. However, the result is that the rope gets shorter and shorter as it wraps around the tree and eventually we can no longer move. In the Amplified Bible, Exodus 1:13 says, *"And the Egyptians reduced the Israelites to severe slavery."* Reduction is a process; it doesn't happen overnight. This does not just happen to us, as individuals. It also happens to us, as congregations.

Many congregations started with a great move of God, maybe a "revival". Blessings were poured out; healing, salvation, growth...then something happens. The excitement of such events is not enough to keep things going. So we spend our energies trying to keep the excitement up, and lose sight of the next phase. Flock and shepherd develop ways to keep the momentum of that growth. Church growth campaigns, the hiring of new leaders, the firing of old ones, building programs, expanding types of ministry, etc. Sounds great...but we need to ask ourselves, "Is there discontentment in the subtle breeze of change we feel?" If there is, it is time for us to surrender to **God's process of planting in us the seeds of revolutionary behavior.** If we are fortunate enough to be part of a revival of some kind, consider searching the heart of God before the erosion of discontentment moves us to make our own decisions of change. We need to ask God for a new brokenness so we can discover the "seed of revolution". **They key to true revival is that every revival has a <u>seed of revolution</u> in it.** It is within these seeds of revolution that the operative destiny of God grows within the hearts of submitted believers, congregations and leaders. **The reason revivals die and a ritual sets in (regardless of the charisma and theological rightness) is because the seeds of revolution were never uncovered.**

The reason Satan fuels our discontentment is so we will start making changes, rather than yielding to God and allowing Him to begin the process of "discovery". The tactic of the enemy is as the scripture said, *to have us "serve with rigor."* The bottom line is that church isn't "fun" anymore. Or more spiritually put, "We are not being as blessed as we used to be." So hardness (mortar) sets in. I remember when I first read these scriptures. The Lord pointed out to me the notion of "rigor" and "mortar". Rigor means "severity and harshness." Mortar is the process of grinding materials to produce brick. Satan fuels our discontentment by causing us to run from the grinding severity we feel. The truth is, *either we can yield our life in a deeper, more committed manner to a loving God, who will gently file away (grind) those areas of our lives that are unproductive and use that process to make brick to build His living sanctuary, or we will yield to our emotional anxiety and allow Satan to grind us into temporary uselessness.*

In the New Testament the word, "mortar" or "mortify," has another nuance to its meaning. The Greek word is "thanatoo," which means, "to become dead." Through the anxieties of the need for change, we gradually allow the passion for purpose and the zeal for destiny to be removed from us. Like life draining from the body, a type of "rigor mortis" sets in and we become hardened to God's desire for "discovery" and revolutionary transformation. The result is an unconscious feeling of resistance to the present situation and a literal stiffness to the wooing of God's Spirit. We are moved to make changes ourselves; we spiritualize them and we may even seek prophetic confirmations of them. But in the end, we are still God's people and He has a purpose and destiny for us. God desires to bring us back to the place where we made the erroneous choices for change and have us yield them to Him. What He will do is begin the uncomfortable process of discovery, similar to what Moses experienced in his Egyptian years in the blended congregational and personal worship culture of fading identity and destiny.

Chapter Three
Revival – The Grindstone

Judg 16:21 Then the Philistines took him and put out his eyes, and brought him down to Gaza. They bound him with bronze fetters, and he became a grinder in the prison. (NKJ)

Before we continue with the notion of Moses' personal revival and the subsequent events that followed, it is absolutely necessary to address those who have labored in the Kingdom of God, whether they are pastors, traveling ministers, or leaders of some kind in God's Kingdom regarding lost vision, moral failure and discouragement. Many have felt the touch of God at one point in time regarding vision and divine purpose for their lives. At times, some have walked in and tasted their anointed potential and the sweetness of a sense of destiny. But at the same time or at a given point in time, even as God's destined servant, the wrestling of life's pressures and the grappling with sinful pleasures caused a fall to the power of guilt, the demons of condemnation and the darkness of personal or ministerial failure. If in some way this has described you, I am convinced that God has put this book in your hand, not only for the entire content, but for this chapter, in particular. You need to know that the weight of guilt is coming to an end, the shackles of condemnation are breaking, and the light of your purpose in life and ministry is coming forth to dispel the darkness of past failures.

If there ever was an example of a believer, who because of failure, lost sight of his vision and purpose in life, it was Samson. Samson was a man who was called and set apart for the purposes of God from the time he was in his mother's womb. He was clearly a man of destiny and like most of us, he was a man of great conflict. It's interesting to note that not only was Samson's life one of personal conflict, but his ministry was ordained to deal with congregational conflict and their contentions with an external enemy. In most cases today, many church leaders are thrown into the crossfire of congregational conflict and at the same time demanded to lead great victories in battle against the onslaughts of external evil.

Like any building structure, its frame and subsequent fabrication is planned within tolerances of weight and distribution. If in the event the tensions are altered, or the weight of responsibility shifts from the designed place to another, eventually the building will collapse. I believe that this is one of the reasons why ministers fall into an absence of a sense of destiny or a convoluted sense of purpose. If they do not fall into some major moral failure, which has a broader reason than just, "The minister messed up because he wasn't living right," discouragement will be the killer. **Many times it is because the minister lives with the silent guilt of not meeting the expectations of the people and the unattained perceived vision of God's will for his or her life.**

In Samson's day, things were no different. The ministerial purpose, pressure and passion of his life had clearly gotten displaced, which eventually lured him into Delilah's lair. Without going into great detail, here was a man of God destined for conflict and anointed to conquer it, but he got caught in the throws of inner conflict because some of his basic needs were not met. He was married to a woman that God appointed for him. He did not get support from his family regarding the marriage because they could not see what God intended. He was betrayed by his father-in-law, who gave Samson's ordained wife to his best man. (See Judges 14.) Because of this inner conflict (which Samson never dealt with), he found himself in the arms of harlots. Eventually, he fell in love with Delilah, who would inevitably cause his demise. But even in Samson worst moments, God was still there.

Every one of us in the Kingdom of God must understand that like Samson, we have been anointed for conflict. We need to realize that while God wants to improve our quality of life and our personal character, we are called to be soldiers. We are commanded to advance His Kingdom against the powers of darkness. We need to realize that the only way we can truly be a success in this life is to champion the inner conflicts that try to keep us from living out our destiny in God. The problem arises because we don't understand when and where the challenge of conflict is appropriate. *Let's simplify. There are two types of external conflict you experience in life: the first, is the kind that you experience because you are advancing the purposes of God's Kingdom. The second, is because you are not advancing the purposes of God's Kingdom.* Either way there is conflict and only one is worth the fight. The problem arises when we stop doing what advances God's purpose for our lives and as a result, shift our focus. It is when we shift the focus that the pressure becomes unbearable and all kinds of subtle fears, guilt and lusts set in. Then what was intended to be an external conflict, becomes an internal one. More importantly, when a conflict takes root internally, usually it is a matter of time until vision is lost and a sense a purpose gives way to weariness in any well doing.

Satan has incapacitated Christian men and women with the darkness of failure, the fetters of depression and the grinding of despair because what they thought was supposed to happen didn't and they got off focus. It became an internal war of failure, or even a sense of betrayal from God. Many church leaders are discouraged because of slow church growth, minimal participation of the congregation in inspired programs, and comparing their success to the success of supposed mentors. Many anointed men and women have left the ministry, or sought sinful means of gratification because their passion for the ministry was not fulfilled. In some cases, leaders have become more discouraged by church growth seminars, rather than encouraged. Why? *Because the focus of a leader's ordained purpose gets convoluted by peer achievement, rather than divine process.* For Samson, God gave him a wife, and he was deprived of her. For believers, we have a vision and it gets convoluted because the process that God chooses to bring it to pass is different than what we expected. We feel deprived of the fulfillment of our vision. The result is that we seek information from others and make them mentors, rather than revelation from God. A mentor is a powerful tool used of God for every believer. But the follower, who in desperation is seeking answers, usually expects too much of the mentor making him or her a little Jesus, rather than allowing that mentor to lead them to a deeper fellowship with Jesus. The Lord put it this way to me one time in prayer, **"A true mentor will lead you to Christ and will light your path. A mentor who has become an idol, will cast a shadow on your path and will make it harder to find your way."** For many leaders, the shadows of the "mega" churches and its leaders have become subtle idols and fuel their discouragement rather than inspire them. This is not necessarily the fault of the "mega" minister (although it can become very easy to think that success came because things were done right, by good marketing techniques, rather than simply by the grace of God). The result is internal struggle and maybe even a self-sabotaging moral failure. The reality is that the weight of focus changed and the internal emotional structure fell.

If you have fallen into sin because of your own lusts getting the best of you due to mishandling of pressure or you have unknowingly let the success of others become an idol and cast a shadow on your vision and purpose, I have good news for you! You cannot fall so low, where God cannot pick you up. You cannot sin so terribly where God cannot forgive you. You cannot fail to fulfill your purpose, where God cannot empower you again.

The days of roller coaster Christianity are over! That is when you win a victory and then plummet into dryness or failure shortly thereafter, repeating the cycle over and over. When you live a roller coaster life, eventually like a roller coaster, you run out of momentum and stop pursuing your higher calling. The life of Samson teaches us a very profound lesson and gives us an even greater hope. ***Our greatest success can come from our worst failures.***

The bottom line is that many of us, because of these issues and others, wind up in the land of Gaza. Gaza, extracted from the Hebrew means, "The Land of Harsh Circumstances." We may have found ourselves unfulfilled in ministry (or in some other area of life) and in seeking a sense of fulfillment, we left where we needed to be and wandered into the land of harsh circumstances. *(Keep in mind that we are destined for conflict, so just because we are in harsh circumstances doesn't mean we are out of focus.)* The problem arises when we are in the land of harsh circumstances with a hazy vision, the results can be discouragement, depression *or Delilah.*

Like Samson, many leaders wandered into a Delilah's lair. It was there, through sin and condemnation, that his source of strength was cut off and the vision of his eyes gouged out. It was there that he wound up chained to the grindstone. For many leaders, you may be in some way there today. You may feel like you have fallen into the power of discouragement, lost your strength or vision, or even fallen into moral failure. You may feel that because of your discouragement, you have been going in circles grinding at life's grindstone. Maybe you feel like your ministry is just going nowhere. Service after service, it's the same thing. Or maybe with every new program the result is the same, all work and no fruit. Maybe you have left the ministry because of weariness and life now just seems to be a hollow rotation of the same scenery, over and over. You may feel like the devil has enslaved you to a grindstone, grinding out some guilt-ridden penance or grinding you with depression and despair. But I have news for you. In Samson's death, he had his greatest victory! The Apostle Paul said:

> **Gal 2:20** *"I have been crucified with Christ; it is no longer I who live, but Christ lives in me; and the life which I now live in the flesh I live by faith in the Son of God, who loved me and gave Himself for me. (NKJ)*

The devil may think he has you in the land of harsh circumstances, darkened with failure, chained with depression, and grinding at the mill of despair. But God is saying, "Man of God, Woman of God! You've got the devil right where you want him!" You may think that you were going around in circles and the devil had you. But while you were going around in circles, your hair was growing out, just like Samson's. That whole time, God was working in Samson a depth of repentance that would give him the greatest victory his life could obtain. In the same way, God has been working in your life a cry to Himself that will change you forever. Each time your heart cries out to God, your spiritual strength (like Samson's hair) grows a little more. In other words, your anointing has been subtly increasing as you have been grinding away any selfish ambition. Can you hear your heart? "I am anointed of God, destined to conquer the conflicts of life with a destiny to crush the power of darkness."

Physically, Samson was blind, but his vision in God was clearer than it had ever been before. He was so clear about his purpose and destiny that his life no longer mattered. The man, who the devil intended to break, became the man who broke the shrine of the devil. The man, who allowed the grinding of lust to crush him, became the man who would grind to rubble his enemy. So Samson took his left hand, put it to one pillar of the temple and took his right hand, put it to the other pillar of the temple and with the resolve of death, applied such pressure that destroyed the enemy of God's people. He fulfilled his calling and purpose!

God has been working in your life the "resolve of death" (embracing the reality of being crucified in Christ), not just theologically or intellectually crucified with Christ, but resolved to that truth as a reality. Get ready to take your left hand and put it to the pillar of your greatest fears, and to take your right hand to the pillar of self-centered ambitions. Take the strength of your renewed passion for God's purposes, burning from the renewed reality of being crucified in Christ, with your sins being blotted out. Being centered in the living will of God, apply the pressure of your God-given destiny, purpose and anointing. Bring down the kingdom of darkness!

Chapter Four
Revival – The Awakening

Exod 2:10 And the child grew, and she brought him to Pharaoh's daughter, and he became her son. So she called his name Moses, saying, "Because I drew him out of the water." (NKJ)

It is evident from the standpoint of scripture that Moses was a man of destiny and purpose. However, we may take this reality for granted. While we read through the first two chapters of the book of Exodus (for many people in less than ten minutes), we take in the facts stated and quickly move on to the "good parts". However, it is within these first chapters of the book, that the entire process of Moses becoming the man of God he was destined to be is outlined.

First, we must remember that Moses only knew of his life and the world on the basis of how he was raised. He did not know the details of his birth. He did not know that his birth mother placed him into the Nile River to avert Pharaoh's decree of death regarding all the newborn Hebrew males. He also did not know that she nursed him and raised him for the first three months of his life (Acts 7:20-21). What we do know is that for the first 37 to 40 years of his life, he grew as the son of an Egyptian princess. In other words, he was raised with the values, the vision and the perspective (the viewpoint) of an Egyptian. Moses saw the world through the eyes of an Egyptian. For Moses, he was a special child. He was the son of an Egyptian princess and taught by the supreme of the intelligencia. His playground was the court of Pharaoh's palace and his future as potential Pharaoh was marked. Yet, during that 40-year period, something was stirring deep within him. You can imagine the questions, "Mother, why am I called Moses, 'One drawn out of the water?'" "Grandfather, why am I circumcised? I hear the Hebrews do this to their sons as a dedication to their God and His covenant." Can you imagine their answers; "You are our miracle son. You were sent down the Nile River to us by Ra, lord of the gods," his Egyptian mother might have said. "Never, compare yourself the to lowly Hebrews, they are nothing more than savage slaves, eating from our land like wild dogs," his Grandfather, Pharaoh, might have stated.

While many of us we recognize that the Hebrew people were severely enslaved by Pharaoh and Egypt, what we don't realize is that Moses was in worse shape. The children of Israel understood and recognized they were in bondage. The man of God, Moses, was enslaved in the most extreme of ways; **he was possessed by his oppressor, and saw the world through his overlord's eyes.** *Moses did not realize he was in the clutches of bondage.* For Moses, a rouse to a new paradigm had to occur. There had to come to a rude, yet wonderful awakening. Moses had to discover **who he was in truth** and **deal with the consequences of that discovery.** (This is the paradox of God's messenger; he is called to be the deliverer of God's people and yet he is raised by the oppressor.)

As Christians, many times we live our lives praying for freedom from sins, afflictions and oppressions, but never recognizing the source of our struggle. *The most common source is the bondage of a broken identity and the enslavement of a "pre-sculptured vision" of our destiny.* By "pre-sculptured vision," I mean to say that many men and women of God see their purpose and destiny in life from the basis of those they admire and glean. In other words, we see our future by the successful accomplishments of those who went before us. For example, if we are called to pastor a church, we tend to envision what our future looks like on the modeling of other successful pastors and leaders, especially our mentors and heroes. (This same principle applies to every aspect of life.) However, the great church leaders, inventors and creators of the past *did not "sculpt their vision" based on their predecessors accomplishments. They discovered vision through "the awakening" of who they were and what they were called to accomplish.* A true mentor (father-like one in the life of an individual) understands how to assist the process of discovery and awakening in a person. The result is that the individual being mentored becomes their own person prepared to father their own family, rather than trying to live life in the shadow of the success of their mentor. When a mentored man or woman of God comes to this realization, he or she can look at the lives of those leaders and mentors and see the hidden workings of God in their lives that achieved revolutionary success. In the end, whether parts of their destiny and vision looked like what anyone else's did no longer becomes the focus. Instead the focus is becoming the person they were called and destined to be. The conclusion is that the ministry born within and proceeding from that person, is unique in its own right and capable of making a significant contribution to the church at large.

Like Moses, what we rarely come to realize is that the areas needing change are the ones *beyond* our paradigm. In short, we are in bondage because of the way we see the world around us and how we fit in that point of view. **True vision is not just a dream for the future,** *but how we see the present around us bending and conforming to whom and what God has destined us to be.* In reality, most of the time we see ourselves bending to circumstances and trying to work within their frame, rather than the reality of God's Word and bringing forth a supernatural dynamic to change the world around us…a dynamic called, "revolution". To get to the point, for us to truly be free, we must face and answer the most frightening two questions that anyone can ask, "Who am I?" and "Why am I here?" Only in the revealed truth of "who we are," can we be free to know why we are here and what our future holds.

Recently my wife, Karen, and I participated in a monthly community healing and worship service in our city at the local United Methodist Church. After the service, I was contemplating some of the things the Methodist pastor shared with the congregation. He shared out of the book of Acts where the sons of Sceva attempted to cast out a demon from a possessed man. The result was devastating for the sons of this chief priest.

Acts 19:15 And the evil spirit answered and said, "Jesus I know, and Paul I know; but who are you?" (NKJ)

Later that night, the words, *"Jesus I know and Paul I know; but who are you?"* rang in my mind and heart. The issue was not that the demons knew Jesus and Paul, **but that Jesus and Paul knew who they themselves were.** The power to conquer hell is not in how loud we command demons to obey, or how familiar we are with demonology, or if we can speak in tongues. The key to overcoming the powers of darkness solely is to know and understand who God created us to be, which gives us a clear perspective (beyond what we think) into the reality of our divine creation and purpose.

Think of it this way. When Satan tempted Jesus in the wilderness, the real issue was not making bread from stone, or jumping off a cliff and letting angels bear Him up, or even worshipping the devil for the kingdoms of the world. The real issue was what Satan prefaced before each temptation. He said, *"If thou be the Son of God..."* The real issue was, "Do you really know who you are?" Satan knew that if Jesus was unsure about who He was, He would be unsure about His future and insecure about how to deal with the devil. Satan knew that if He could get Jesus to question His identity, it would be a sure win for Hades.

The same is true with the case of Moses and with you and me. Satan indoctrinates us from an early age, helping shape our emotional and mental structure to behave in a certain matter. The effect is that our understanding is distorted, contrary to "who we truly are," resulting in dysfunctional conduct and a contorted paradigm. Yet all the while we believe we're fine. We say things like: "It's those people that have the problem." In our lives we may become influential in the community or our sphere of employment. But regardless of how well off or how needy we are, we still need to awaken to our true identity, the person created by God's Divine Design. Regardless of Moses' schooling, regardless of his status as the son of the Princess of Egypt, and regardless of his clothing and the friends he grew up with, down deep he was a man created by God for that season and for a divine purpose.

As men and women born of God's Spirit, regardless of age or status, God has marked our lives for a specific purpose. Because of this, many times Satan does all he can to distort and disfigure our *personal and world-view*. When we come to Christ (having received new life in the Spirit), we are much like young Moses, who after a period of years, begin to feel a stirring deep within. This is where the winds of change began to blow. Even though everything (our environment, denomination, or non-denomination, well meaning friends, and so on) tells us "who we should be" and "what we are supposed to do in life," down deep within the awakening to divine design begins as God blows upon us the winds of change.

Exod 2:11-12 *11 Now it came to pass in those days, when Moses was grown, that he went out to his brethren and looked at their burdens. And he saw an Egyptian beating a Hebrew, one of his brethren. 12 So he looked this way and that way, and when he saw no one, he killed the Egyptian and hid him in the sand. (NKJ)*

Over the process of time, Moses began to realize his kindred and his origin. But it was through "divine conflict" God drew Moses out and truly awakened him to who He called him to be. On that day, Moses left the comforts of his *world-view* and **"...*went out* to his brethren *and looked...*"** Think of all the times that Moses saw the Hebrew slaves toiling in their bondage. The situation did not change, but something within Moses did. God began to stir within Moses his true identity and something started to give way. Something began to break forth. That something was so powerful, that for the first time in his life, **he went out *beyond his personal and world-view and "looked."*** When he did, he caught a glimpse of who he was and what he was called to be, and it moved him to radical action. What was the motivating power that arose from within Moses and changed the way he looked at himself, the world and his future? The following scripture from the New Testament exposes us to the center of this seed in the midst of Moses' personal revival.

> ***Mark 1:40-42*** *40 Then a leper came to Him, imploring Him, kneeling down to Him and saying to Him, "If You are willing, You can make me clean." 41 And Jesus, moved with compassion, put out His hand and touched him, and said to him, "I am willing; be cleansed." 42 As soon as He had spoken, immediately the leprosy left him, and he was cleansed. (NKJ)*

Many times throughout the Gospels, we see this phrase or a similar phrase, *"And Jesus was moved with compassion..."* Every time Jesus took action, He said that He did what He saw the Father do and said what He heard the Father say. If that were the case, then the essence of the Father's nature and heart is *compassion*. It was *compassion* that moved Jesus to heal, to cast out demons, and ultimately take the most spiritual and revolutionary step that any living being could make, the sacrificial offering of He Himself on the cross. *What is compassion?* It is actually quite simple to define. *Just look at our suffering Savior in torment upon the cross, and look into His eyes as He willfully submits to death as a sin offering, for both you and for me.* Hear His voice cry in agony to His heavenly Father, "Father forgive them, they don't know what they are doing," while His heart shouts to us even louder, "I love you so, that my passion brings my life to this point and moves me beyond the portals of hell." Think of the three days and nights in the lonely darkness of the cold grave. The voice of that same compassion roared through the power of death and resurrected a dead tormented body in a tomb. Hear the burst of heavenly compassion as the sealed tomb breaks... the stone rolls from its holding place and the glorified Christ appears. Look again into those same eyes and see the fire of His compassion saying, "My love for you is so full, that my passion encompasses my whole being bringing me forth from death in newness of eternal life to set you free."

When Moses went out among his brethren on that day, he looked beyond his normal point of view, because he saw with eyes that took him past his usual emotional, intellectual and spiritual boundaries. For a brief moment Moses saw with the eyes of his Creator from the very center of his being. He saw with the eyes of *compassion* and was moved by it to radical action.

Compassion is two words, "compass" and "passion." It means to completely surround (compass) with desire (passion). Moses saw, the oppressor crushing the oppressed. Thus, so being moved with compassion, completely encompassed with the desire of God, Moses delivered the Hebrew slave from the Egyptian. But this process of "drawing out" did not stop there for Moses. God drew him again into the heat of "divine conflict," to bring Moses to another point of revival and awakening.

> ***Exod 2:13-14*** *13 And when he went out the second day, behold, two Hebrew men were fighting, and he said to the one who did the wrong, "Why are you striking your companion?" 14 Then he said, "Who made you a prince and a judge over us? Do you intend to kill me as you killed the Egyptian?" So Moses feared and said, "Surely this thing is known!" (NKJ)*

In the first conflict, Moses was awakened through the compassion of God by seeing the suffering of his people. In that moment while Moses was encompassed by God's desire, he also caught a glimpse of who he was. He tasted the reality that he was the deliverer of his people. He was awakened to the fact that not only was he a Hebrew, but that he was the deliverer of the Hebrews. In short, he saw "who he was," and "what he was called to be." This motivated Moses to step out again.

In the case of the second conflict, God had to bring Moses to a rude awakening. As Moses once again saw with the eyes of compassion, he stepped into the middle of a conflict, this time with two Hebrews. When he attempted to stop the fight, one of the Hebrew men shouted, *"Who made you a prince and a judge over us?"* To put it another way, "Who do you think you are!" It was the same old question that Satan demanded of Jesus during his temptations, and the demons in the possessed man demanded of the sons of Sceva. The reality was that Moses couldn't answer the question. What he also did not realize was that the Hebrew men gave him the answer. He was to be the ruler of God's people. The only difference in this case was that it was not the devil who was asking the question; it was God. The result was that Moses retreated in fear. Remember in our example of Jesus, that compassion moved Him to "self-sacrifice." Moses, at this point, withdrew from his identity (which was divinely connected to the compassion of God) and became once again "self-centered." In other words, Moses brief revival had come and now had gone. But God had a method to this challenge. God put Moses in a position where he only had a glimpse of his identity and not the fullness of "who he was", or the depth of his calling; but that was enough to begin the process to bring Moses from revival to revival and eventually, to birth revolution. On top of this, God saw to it that Moses could not go back to living in his old Pharaoh-infested world-view. In reality, while Moses killed the Egyptian and freed the Hebrew slave, he also extinguished the Egyptian within himself. Moses could not go back; he had a glimpse of who he was. But he also was too afraid and unknowing to go forward. Moses ran into the desert.

Like many of us believers, God draws us into a "divine conflict." A conflict intended to draw us out. There, we catch a glimpse of our identity and destiny, and attempt to step out and take action. But in our immaturity we do not know how respond to God when he asks us, "Who do you say you are?" Because of this awakening, we know we cannot retreat back to the way life use to be. Yet, at the same time (and in most cases) we are afraid of the turbulence this new horizon brings us. Caught in the remains of a divine conflict and a brief revival, we run to the long journey of the desert. Our spiritual walk is dry. It seems as though the moving of God's Spirit is rarely if ever taking place. We secretly long to have that glimpse again. What we don't realize is that God is bringing us through the desert on purpose. It is there in the desert (the dry times) where He works in us depth of desire.

Like Moses, when God first draws us out, we run from conflict, only to find ourselves parched and dry in the desert. Many of us are experiencing dryness today because we are running from divine conflicts. God is challenging us, bringing us to the greatness of His divine design. In the midst of your driest moment, what do you long for? Chances are, within that flash of remembrance is the glimpse of your identity and destiny in God.

Chapter Five
Revival – The Refreshing

Exod 2:15-17 15 When Pharaoh heard of this matter, he sought to kill Moses. But Moses fled from the face of Pharaoh and dwelt in the land of Midian; and he sat down by a well. 16 Now the priest of Midian had seven daughters. And they came and drew water, and they filled the troughs to water their father's flock. 17 Then the shepherds came and drove them away; but Moses stood up and helped them, and watered their flock. (NKJ)

During the desert journey from Egypt to Midian, God was preparing a "well of refreshing" for Moses. God did not intend for Moses to go through the "desert of longing and desire" to dry out and quit. He fully intended for Moses' longing to become a thirst that the "well of refreshing" would quench. But to receive from the *well of refreshing,* we must draw and be drawn out once again.

Moses was about to experience one of the most important revivals of his life. Here he was, once again drinking at the wells of God's Spirit. His thirst was being quenched. Like Moses, after a great longing, God leads us to a marvelous refreshing, revitalization and revival, in the truest sense of the word. But once again it brings with it a glimpse of our identity and destiny. As Moses is sitting by this wonderful well, shepherdesses arrive. Their intention is to water their flocks, but as they draw from the well, shepherds arrive and conflict breaks out. The shepherds attempt to drive away the shepherdesses. Once again, Moses is *drawn out,* and finds himself in the middle of the conflict. The scripture said, *"...but Moses stood up, and helped them water their flock."* **Not only has God's well refreshed Moses, but it also has revived him to the point where he is able to stand in conflict and draw from that well, to minister to others.** This time Moses is not running from the conflict; he is standing in the midst of it and going beyond his *previous* personal and worldview. Moses' identity and destiny is subtly coming forth as a natural expression of his existence. The only problem was that Moses did not recognize it.

There are many Christians today who are crying out for God to show them who they are and what their future holds, and all the while it is right under their noses. They are serving in the church, ministering in different capacities, and yet they are uncomfortable. Unfortunately what happens is that they find that the ministry in which they are involved seems to perpetuate conflict, resulting in a roller coaster ride of discomfort. Many times when God is confronting us with "who we are," we feel like we are in perpetual conflict. This is no accident. The reason is that the *well of refreshing* is placed in the land of *Midian*. In the Hebrew, Midian means *strife or conflict*. God knew exactly what it would take to develop Moses and to develop us into the men and women of God we are destined to be. So He put a *well of refreshing* in a very strategic place, in the *land of conflict and strife*. The purpose of the *well of refreshing* is to keep us vital while in the conflict so we can go on to discovery. The only problem is our approach to such revivals.

Like in the days of Moses, Christians today do not understand the value of their revivals (or wells of refreshing). These revivals usually last longer than just a brief awakening, like in Moses first encounter. These revivals have a tremendous amount of power and have the ability to move us from a point of receiving to a point of ministry, like with Moses and the shepherdesses. The only problem is that while the revival empowers us to stay in the conflict, we believe we have reached our destination. We blame the bulk of our inner, and sometimes outer conflict on the devil, and we call it "spiritual warfare" or give it some other pious meaning. We assume that the struggle exists because we are in the middle of the spiritual "what's happening now." Think of it; this revival brings Moses many blessings. First, he meets and is accepted into a spiritual family. Reuel (which means, "friend of God") is the priest of Midian. Wow! How many Christians today are excited with the idea that they are part of a fellowship whose pastor (or priest) is the *friend of God.* Can't you hear it, "You have to go to this special meeting; it's like a well of refreshing. When the minister preaches, he is like the personal friend of God!" But it doesn't stop there! "During this revival, I met my wife-to-be, Birdie (Zipporah), we got married last week. On top of that, I got a new job working for the ministry, helping tend the pastor's flock." Sound familiar yet? It's exactly what happened to Moses.

We need to realize what God is intending and what he is attempting to draw us into. First, we need to recognize that **the well of refreshing does not bring lasting change.** It only refreshes. Second, **the blessings of the present may have the future written on them, but that doesn't mean we have arrived.** The *well of refreshing* is not our identity or our destiny; it is a tool of God to bring us to a place of discovery in divine conflict.

Exod 2:18-21 18 When they came to Reuel their father, he said, "How is it that you have come so soon today?" 19 And they said, "An Egyptian delivered us from the hand of the shepherds, and he also drew enough water for us and watered the flock." 20 So he said to his daughters, "And where is he? Why is it that you have left the man? Call him, that he may eat bread." 21 Then Moses was content to live with the man, and he gave Zipporah his daughter to Moses. (NKJ)

In Moses' case, like most of us, as the scripture says, *"Moses was content to live with the man..."* The incriminating word is, ***"content."*** The Hebrew root word means, "to be slack," in some cases, "to be foolish." Many of us believers are *content* to live in *conflict* as long as our local revival, *well of refreshing* and *friend of God* is around to give us a boost. In some cases we will even leave the congregation God has assigned us, because the church on the other side of town appears to be a *well of refreshing,* while our church appears to be a desert. (We will deal with this in the next chapter.) The enigma of the situation is that we desire to park ourselves in the midst of revival, but in our subtle contentment we become slack and maybe even foolish regarding the purposes of God.

Moses did not realize what God was actually doing in his life. It wasn't about living near the *well of refreshing,* or his new bride, or his new career, and getting victory in the midst of conflict. Actually, it was about the bread he was offered by the man of God from *the table of discovery.* Reuel said, *"Call him, that he may eat bread!"* Why? Because regardless how long Moses drank of the well, **he still looked like an Egyptian.** The daughters of Reuel said, *"An Egyptian delivered us from the hands of the shepherds..."* Yes, even after the long journey through the *desert of longing and desire,* even after attending the revival at the *well of refreshing,* **Moses still looked like an Egyptian.** Even though the Egyptian within was extinguished before the desert, he still looked like an Egyptian in his external expression. Now God was about to walk Moses through the arduous task of not just looking beyond into a new paradigm (a new personal and worldview), but of becoming the man that lies *beyond that view.*

Many times we, as followers of Christ, catch a glimpse of who and what we are and assume that we are ready for the fullness of our identity and destiny. But in actuality, we may have extinguished the Egyptian (the old man within), but now we must become something new, not just on the inside, but in both internal and external expression. Like Adam, who was lifeless, and needed God to breathe in him the breath of Life, we, too (after we have extinguished the old paradigm and the man who lived in it) must allow God to breathe in us His breath of Life. It was that same "breath of Life" that gave Adam's soul animation and expression. This doesn't come as easily as one may think. Unlike the quick and revitalizing *well of refreshing,* the *table of discovery* is a slow consumption of truth, which we assimilate and which becomes part of who we are. It gradually prepares us for the forthcoming life-changing encounter with God that will produce spiritual revolution in us and in the world around us. In short, if God were to tell Moses his destiny and tell him to go back to Egypt in his current condition, it would be disaster for both Moses and God's plan. Consider this: Moses, looking like an Egyptian, walks into the camp of the Hebrews and says, "I am your new prophet." What do you think their response would be? Maybe, "You, son of an Egyptian princess! We'll have you know that NO Egyptian prince will be our prophet!" (I would imagine you could add more dialogs to this losing proposition of Moses.) But it would not stop there. Can you imagine him entering Pharaoh Rameses' court, "Moses, my brother, since our grandfather has passed on into the next life, I have assumed the throne. But please, this request about letting the Hebrew slaves go is ridiculous. First, they are not YOUR people; look at yourself in the mirror. Don't you still express the heart of a Pharaoh's son?" Needless to say, on both accounts Moses would be embarrassed in the very least, or at worst, killed by the Hebrews for blasphemy, or even executed by Rameses for treason.

It took almost another forty years of Moses living in conflict, seasoned with the waters of revival and eating at the table of discovery for him to come to the point of becoming the man of God he was destined to be. During this time, God was at work preparing Moses for another journey. It was during this time Moses began to realize he did not fit in.

Exod 2:22 And she bore him a son, and he called his name Gershom; for he said, "I have been a stranger in a foreign land." (NKJ)

The idea of Moses having a sense of displacement is twofold. Moses now understood that he was *"a stranger in a foreign land,"* when living in Egypt. But now, he also began to recognize that he did not belong in the land of Midian either. There was tremendous unrest in Moses. Many Christians today are in this quandary. Many know that they are not of the world anymore and may even have a picture of their identity and destiny in life. But if you were to ask them, "Are you really happy about the way life is right now? Are you at total peace with your walk with God? Do you believe you are living in the potential that God has destined for you to walk in?" The honest believer would probably answer, "No." Why? Because God has a greater place in this hour for His man, His woman, and His Church.

For Moses the unrest became so desperate, that he found himself unknowingly wandering, flock and all, away from the land of Midian, the *well of refreshing* and the *table of discovery*. **He found himself back in the desert, dry and parched, ministry and all.**

Chapter Six
Revolution – The Burning

Exod 3:1 Now Moses was tending the flock of Jethro his father-in-law, the priest of Midian. And he led the flock to the back of the desert, and came to Horeb, the mountain of God. (NKJ)

It is interesting to note that Moses' father-in-law's name went through a metamorphosis. Revival started out for Moses as Reuel, *the friend of God*. Now that name transformed into Jethro, meaning, *abundance* and *excellence*. In other words, this process brought great satisfaction, abundance and entitlement. But in the core of what had grown so wonderful, now became unsettling. In this personal and spiritual growth Moses found himself back in the same desert as before. But this time, it was different. First he had the responsibility of all he had learned and lived. Second, as the waters of revival became insufficient regarding his ultimate purpose, he became desperate and desolate. Now and only now, was he in the place where God could bring forth what He had intended from the beginning. Moses found himself at the base of Mount Horeb, which is later called *the Mount of God*.

Horeb, in Hebrew means, *desolate*. I remember that when I came to this passage the first time, I asked the Lord what it meant. I said, "Lord, why Horeb, a desolate place? Why would You, the Creator of the universe, be found in such a horrible, dry, empty place?" It was then that the Holy Spirit impressed on me the picture of this land. He pointed out to me that there was virtually no life, vegetation, trees nor fruit. It was then, in His still small voice that He said, "I abide where nothing else can exist. *I make My home where your pride, your fears, your attitude and your ambitions cannot survive."* It was then that I realized that the way to our true identity and destiny in God is when all our self-centered, ambitious, egocentric, self-absorbed focus is dead. It is only when we realize intellectually, emotionally and spiritually, that **He is truly the only source of all life** including identity, ministry, future and destiny. It is only then that we are ready and completely capable of doing what God has always intended for us to do. It is only then that we can turn the course of our life from "regular" to "revolutionary," from *revival* to *revolution,* and from natural to supernatural. We may have thought that the beauty of revival (the *well of refreshing*) was the key, but it was only a catalyst. The reality is in Horeb, the desolate place, where we discover who we are and what we are called to be.

Many men and women of God, church leaders, pastors and theologians are in this place right now. I know of many appointed men and women leading worship services, experience anointings, healings, and so on, but they still go home empty and dry. Why? Because the wooing of God is drawing them out to His Mountain, His Dwelling, *Horeb,* the place of desolation and resolution, the birthplace of *revolution.*

Exod 3:2-3 2 And the Angel of the LORD appeared to him in a flame of fire from the midst of a bush. So he looked, and behold, the bush was burning with fire, but the bush was not consumed. 3 Then Moses said, "I will now turn aside and see this great sight, why the bush does not burn." (NKJ)

At this point, Moses was experiencing something that would change his life forever. He was about to do what few of us realize that we need to do; instead we resist with great religiosity. When all the natural and supernatural wisdom would say, "Moses you are in a desert place in life. You need to return to the *well of refreshing* and drink of the Lord. You need to go back from where you came and humble yourself and drink," God had another idea. The angel of the Lord appeared in a *burning bush.* Think about this; you're in the back part of the desert, which means you been traveling for awhile. Along with you is your flock, or ministry.

The weight of responsibility here is not just about you, it is now about all that you have been building in your life (family, vocation ministry, etc.) and consequently you now find it all in dryness. First of all, the sheep are complaining, "Baah! Why have you brought us to this place? Where are the cool still waters? Baah! We're hungry and we haven't been fed. There's no green pastures here!" So you say, "I know! I know! But for some strange reason, I still believe this is the way for us to go." **Finally, when you are so dry and weary, and when you feel like you cannot go any further, you see off in the distance, a *burning bush*.** Here is the next ridiculous thing to do. Rather than avoid more heat and dryness from the flame, and rather than turn back and run for the *wells of refreshing,* **you turn and approach the fire.** You welcome it. Your attitude is like a man or woman who is slowly losing their common sense. The blaze you see with your eyes is almost soothing, and the heat rather then harsh, is pleasant. Then you hear a strong, yet gentle voice, "Moses, Moses." Up until this point, God never called Moses by name. God had been working in his life, from revival to revival (refreshing to refreshing) in the midst of family, ministry and business, **but now God calls him by name.**

For this event to take place, something significant had to occur. The scripture states, *"Moses said, 'I will now turn aside and see...'"* Once again, Moses goes beyond his normal perspective and point of view. Rather than take the easy natural way by saying, "It is so hot out here that even the bushes are burning..." He sees something in the midst of the blaze that is almost enchanting. He *saw* that the bush was not consumed. To amplify the point, this could not have happened in a glance. In a glance this would have looked like any other burning bush under the hot sun. Moses must have looked at it from a distance with some intensity. After watching the bush blaze Moses recognized that it was not being consumed. It was this "stretch of vision," (going beyond the normal, even average spiritual paradigm) that Moses moved to take a closer look. **The bible clearly states that** after Moses turned aside to see, **then** the Lord called to Him. In other words, not only was Moses stretching himself to see beyond what would be "spiritually common"; he was now comparing this discovery with his normal way of thinking. This is very difficult for us, as Christians, to do. To make an **objective comparison to our normal way of thinking,** even spiritually, **is uncommon.** Most of the time, we expend a lot of effort defending what we believe or think, rather than stretching ourselves. This is why denominations exist today. We like what is comfortable, common and that which takes the least amount of effort. From the inquisition to the present day, it's the same. A couple of years ago, revival broke out in a nearby city. It was wonderful. God was moving and many were refreshed and touched. The only problem was that after a while we, in the church world, began to do what we always do, "Hey, are you going to go to the great refreshing?" as if to imply that if you are anywhere else you are not being refreshed. Needless to say, people began to leave their churches and attend services at the revival site. Rather than take what God was doing and apply it to their lives so they could bless the ministry they were a part of, many left their assignments at their churches and changed membership. Now you may say, "Pastor, please! It has taken a lot of effort to get where I am in the Lord." That may be true; I know I can say the same thing. But in reality, it is not you or me that has expended the real effort; it has been the untiring work of the Holy Spirit. The fact is, we resist His wooing more often than we all would like to admit. How many of us, in the Christian world, expend our energies defending doctrines and fortifying what we believe is God's moving (entrenching ourselves in biblical or spiritual rightness), *rather than humbling ourselves with the compassion of the Lord and loving like Jesus.* Why? To put it as the Lord put it to me, "John, in your life you may need healing of your emotions, the transforming of your mind, and the education of My Word and Spirit; but ultimately that is not enough. **Emotions can be healed, minds can be changed,** *but "the will" can only be broken."*

At the *burning bush* Moses experienced what we have a real tough time with. It's called, *"brokenness."* It was only when he realized something was completely different (in what could have looked "ordinary" at a quick glance), could God call him by name. To put it another way, Moses had nothing left. He left Egypt, which started this whole process. He now was (in the very least emotionally and mentally), empty and dry regarding family, business, ministry and children. Everything that mattered to him for almost eighty years of his life was now hollow. **There was nothing left, except God and himself.** It was in this situation that Moses took the best possible step. He turned to see what was different, rather than complaining that everything was the same and going nowhere. When we do this, God like a flaming blaze awaits us, burning to call our name.

Chapter Seven
Revolution – The Transformation

Exod 3:4-6 4 So when the LORD saw that he turned aside to look, God called to him from the midst of the bush and said, "Moses, Moses!" And he said, "Here I am." 5 Then He said, "Do not draw near this place. Take your sandals off your feet, for the place where you stand is holy ground." 6 Moreover He said, "I am the God of your father-- the God of Abraham, the God of Isaac, and the God of Jacob." And Moses hid his face, for he was afraid to look upon God. (NKJ)

At this point in the process of Moses' transformation is when it reaches the pinnacle. This is where God and Moses would *write in indelible ink*, the identity and future of both the man and the ministry. Here at the *burning bush* is where God would reckon with Moses regarding his anointing and his character. Here is where Moses, in light of the dealings of God, would set his course to the future embracing both notable victories and eminent failures. Like Moses, for us to do this we must understand that *"brokenness"* in the life of an individual, is not the beginning of an impeccable walk with God, a skilled maturity in the craft of ministry, or even a new level of holiness; it is simply what it is, *"brokenness"*. **It is the reckoning central act of oneself embracing God solely, and the beginning of the process of becoming a reflection of that which we have embraced.**

In truth, many of us fear *brokenness* like we would fear a terminal disease. The idea of recognizing that in this life as we know it, there is nothing that can truly fulfill us, is a very frightening thing. The process of coming to that realization is even more alarming. Many times we respond from a theological standpoint (presupposing that the standpoint is rational), rather than responding from a relational one. Many times we simply regurgitate the theological concept that Christ is our fulfillment, but coming to that dynamic reality in personal expression and experience is another issue. **For that matter, coming to that recognition, in the truest sense, is the beginning of Christian living and true Christian ministry.** But unfortunately, we as Christians spend most of our lives resisting *brokenness* through theological correctness, spiritual gymnastics, material "breakthroughs," and acts of service. Eventually all these will get dry and empty. It is here, in the dryness, where things can get dangerous for us regardless of circumstantial outcome, miracle, or lack thereof. It is here, in our recognition of empty fulfillment where we feel we need to leave our marriage to explore "another" intimate partner, another career, another church, another seminar, and so on. Sometimes we believe we have outgrown our church or our friends because we see them as a restraint, hindering us from our "breakthrough." It is at this point in our lives that we may do as the Israelites did, when God brought them out of Egypt to Mount Horeb. While Moses was high up the mountain seeking God, they were in the *"valley of brokenness"* creating for themselves their own god and yielding to riotous living (See all of Exodus 32).

Exod 32:4-5 4 And he received it at their hand, and fashioned it with a graving tool, and made it a molten calf: and they said, These are thy gods, O Israel, which brought thee up out of the land of Egypt. 5 And when Aaron saw (this), he built an altar before it; and Aaron made proclamation, and said, To-morrow shall be a feast to Jehovah. (ASV)

In the modern church, when we come to the *"valley of brokenness,"* we may not fall into some form of immorality (although it can happen as we stated earlier), but into what I call, **"revival revelry."** Similar to our previous examples with Moses at the *"well of refreshing,"* here the children of Israel wind up in compromise. The biggest offense was not the immoral behavior, which could have been forgiven through sacrificial worship, but the building of the altar before which they create a golden calf and name it, "Jehovah." In short, as God leads His people to Mount Horeb (the *valley of brokenness*), many times we **create** revival. Many times we create it in the like manner of what we genuinely experienced in the past. The real danger arises out of the fact that God is not moving to bring revival, but revolution and revolutionaries. So what happens when we resist God's move toward brokenness and revolution? **We create our own revival and *revel in it.*** Worse yet, as stated in the scripture, ***"...he built an altar before it; and Aaron made a proclamation, and said, Tomorrow shall be a feast to Jehovah."*** Rather than being broken and becoming a congregation of revolutionary proportion, the children of Israel **created their own revival, and named the golden calf, "Jehovah."** Herein lies the dilemma with some of our revivalists and their followers. We call our created revival revelry, "the Spirit." In our *inflexible* attempt to respond to God's courtship to *brokenness,* we cling to the most recent music, message, minister and/or organizational association. We build an altar to "our spiritual replacement" for God's surgery and name it "a move of God." **In addition, to be consistent with our *resistance* to brokenness (in spite of the fact that God delivered us from our own personal Egypt), we build our fabricated revival using the spoils God gave us when He delivered us from the Egypt we were in.** (According to Exodus 32:2-4, Aaron told the people to take off their earrings and jewelry to create the golden calf. In Exodus 3:21-22, we are told that the children of Israel were given these items as the spoils of deliverance!)

As stated earlier, we have to "go beyond and look." For us to move past our normal point of view, we have to first be made aware that God is not limited by our point of view and for that matter, sees the world through an Alpha and Omega position. We must always remember that *we are the ones with the limitation* and that limitation is what we use to <u>create</u> graven images.

When Moses came to his point of brokenness, God did five things:

1. **"He called Moses by name."** This is the center and foundation of all the subsequent events. When God calls a person by name, instantly an understanding of identity begins to settle. This was one of the reasons Jesus emphasized to Simon:

   Matt 16:17-18 *17 Jesus answered and said to him, "Blessed are you, Simon Bar-Jonah, for flesh and blood has not revealed this to you, but My Father who is in heaven. 18 "And I also say to you that you are Peter, and on this rock I will build My church, and the gates of Hades shall not prevail against it. (NKJ)*

   When Simon recognized that there was no other place to go and no one else to follow but the Savior, he was ready to be called by name. This extended beyond salvation and ecclesiastical service into the realization of "personal purpose." Peter was now ready to hear, *"You are Peter (Petros – a piece of a larger rock) and on this rock (Petra – a massive rock) [the revelation that I am the Christ], I will build My Church..."* At this point Peter received that he had a purpose and was a part, "a piece," of the "massive rock" of God's Divine plan. Peter would then shortly thereafter complete his process of *brokenness* by discovering his own point of desolation when he wept bitterly after denying Christ.

   We must reconcile within our hearts that this calling by name is more than a call to ministry or a commission to service. For many Christians, this experience occurs long after we have begun our ministry life. **This calling by name is the foundation of the revolutionary life.** It is the realization of who we are. Not by the wonders of self-centered discovery, but the discovery that "self" is vastly insufficient and in that helplessness, God speaks our name.

2. **"He transformed the way he walked."** When God called Moses by name, a second event immediately happened. God said, *"Take off your sandals, the place you are standing is holy*

ground." In addition to the standard custom of that day (which according to commentaries is much like taking off the hat today, being a gesture of respect and submission), another inference can be applied. *"Moses, take off your present walking shoes, because when we finish here, you will leave this holy place and **never walk the same.**"* Another place where this occurs is in the life of Jacob. It was after he wrestled with the angel of the Lord all night, that he was called by his ordained name, "Israel." It was through the wrestling that *the seed of revolution* was planted in Jacob. He, too, after receiving his identity from the Lord, no longer walked the same; he walked with a limp. With each step, it reminded him of his transformation and his destiny to bring forth a revolutionary nation. Some of us have been through situations were our fears and anger caused us to resist and wrestle with God to the point that we now limp. But the limp (like in the life of Jacob) has become a source of remembrance of our point of transformation, rather than being a sign of our failure to obtain godliness, or our human frailty wrestling for the divine.

When God calls us by name, it is not simply hearing a voice proclaim our birth name, but it is the recognition of what we have longed for throughout the process. **It is the acute awareness and pointed designation that God knows who we are right down to the core. It is the moment of our discovery that in the most intimate places of our heart, God knows where we are in the journey of life.** It is a place of total humility and yet, expectation. When God called, He said that He was the God of his (Moses') "fathers." **The burning bush was and *is* the place of connection with Divine history.** It is in this place of heavenly lineage that Moses would be grounded and anchored. It is in the grounding of Divine history that would give Moses a broad, yet focused picture of his role in the design of redemption. For us, it is a revelation of who we are, not from our recognition of our personal condition, but *it is actually seeing who God always intended for us to be.* It is clarity that we are *a piece of the rock* and part of a vast plan in which God has a very definite purpose and future for us. It is a place of recognition to kinship of God's unfolding plan and it is also a place of recognition to His Kingdom. It is the point, where we see ourselves in the timeline of destiny which has been at work since God spoke of redemption when Mankind fell in the garden. Simultaneously, it is a place of assimilation of the approaching hope of a new future, a new heaven and a new earth. **In the immediate, it is the inner knowing that God ordained our existence long before we were a sparkle in our parent's eye...for such a time as this.** In the case of Moses, when God called him by name, "Moses", the revelation of being "One drawn out," expanded into being the deliverer of *"One drawing out"* God's people from slavery.

3. **"He revealed Himself."** The third aspect of encountering the burning bush, is **the "<u>result</u>" of our brokenness,** which is **"humility,"** *born by God revealing Himself.* Regardless of all the truths we may have heard about our righteousness in Christ, most of the time we approach our self worth focused on the legal merit of God's Word. While it is a very valuable fact for us to know we are legally declared forgiven and righteous, it is another thing to become aware of the Holy presence of the Almighty. For us, at the faint point of brokenness, opening our inner eyes to the Divine (seeing Him), and then by His doing, revealing ourselves in His image; can only result in humility, submissiveness, *and worship.* Whether we recognize that we are legally righteous or not, we will hide our face in worshipful awe because of His greatness and that which He discloses concerning us. The foundation of true biblical humility is not an intellectual knowledge of our legal status in the Kingdom of God, but it is while in our brokenness, we embrace the vision of His presence and embrace the vision He has of us.

4. **"He revealed Moses destiny and purpose."** The forth element that we encounter at this point, is the revelation of our destiny in the plan of God.

   Exod 3:7,8,10 7 *And the LORD said: "I have surely seen the oppression of My people who are in Egypt, and have heard their cry because of their taskmasters, for I know their sorrows. 8 "So I have come down to deliver them out of the hand of the Egyptians... 10 "Come now, therefore, and I will send you to Pharaoh that you may bring My people, the children of Israel, out of Egypt." (NKJ)*

It is one thing to say, "I know God has a plan for me," and another to say, "I know what that plan is." Once we clearly see and hear the revelation of our destiny in God, life doesn't just change; life begins to unfold. It is like pouring liquid down a funnel. Regardless of how turbulent the fluid in the large portion of the funnel, even if the fluid level rises to the top, ultimately it only has one direction to go. Out the appointed way of the spout. Receiving the realization of our destiny transforms our perspective of life into an unchanging focus, much like the funnel. It is not that we become narrow-minded (though we may be accused of such things), but that it becomes truly satisfying for us to walk the straight and narrow road called, "destiny." If we are wise to the process that brought us to this point of *"revolutionary transformation,"* we will never become narrow-minded. Actually, we will become broader in our thinking in both heart and mind because we have learned that God can be found far beyond our point of view and has much to reveal to us. (One of the reasons the Church-world has such problems with unity among the different flavors of tradition and worship is that we believe our point of view is the alpha and omega.) Yet while God has broadened our perspective, the renewed understanding of ourselves and the purposes of God causes us to focus on tomorrow with unwavering ability. To put it another way, there is no turbulence, no person, no situation, no demonic attack, no illness, no financial situation, no depression, no sin, and no life experience that will derail our journey of Divine destiny. The only person or thing that can postpone, hinder or even derail the unfolding journey is ourselves.

Within the revealing of our identity and destiny also comes the unveiling of the most intimate part of God's heart. **He reveals what moves Him.**

Ps 103:7 He made known His ways to Moses, his acts to the children of Israel. (NKJ)

This was not *just* an unveiling of Moses' destiny, but wrapped within the awareness of that destiny was *the heart of God.* Many times we pray that we would be like Jesus. Many times we read the scripture concerning King David and how it says that he was a man after God's heart (1 Sam 13:14) so we pray that we would seek the heart of God. But in order for us to embrace God's heart, we must come in contact with the destiny He has ordained for us. The reason the scripture says that Moses knew God's ways, and the children of Israel only knew His acts, was because of what happened at Mount Horeb.

Exod 3:12 So He said, "I will certainly be with you. And this shall be a sign to you that I have sent you: When you have brought the people out of Egypt, you shall serve God on this mountain." (NKJ)

God told Moses that the sign that his mission was ordained of Him would be that the children of Israel would serve God at the same mountain. In other words, they were to come to the same place of brokenness and revolutionary transformation as Moses had. But unfortunately for the children of Israel, they did not respond as Moses did when they arrived in the valley of the mount. In the case of the Moses, he saw the burning bush and recognized there was something different about what seemed usual. He turned aside to see (went beyond his normal point of view), and allowed God to reveal Himself. But the children of Israel did not. They came to what grew from a burning bush into a blazing mountain, yet they refused to look beyond their own standpoint. Think of it! Moses saw a burning bush, which could have been construed essentially as "ordinary" in the heat of the desert. But here, the children of Israel see an entire mountain in a blaze, with thunder, lighting and a powerful voice that sounded like a trumpet; but they still built an altar, created their own image and named it "Jehovah". *The result was devastating.* From this point on, an entire generation would die before getting an opportunity to enter the Promised Land. When you think about this further, because the people would not look up and change, God allowed Moses to see part of His Glory (which changed Moses countenance), so that the fire of God would now, in the face of Moses, go down the mount and dwell among the people. But rather than the children of Israel looking upon it, they were afraid and had Moses place a veil over himself. Why...?

*Exod 34:30 So when Aaron and all the children of Israel saw Moses, behold, the skin of his face shone, and **they were afraid to come near him.** (NKJ)*

*2 Cor 3:13-14 & 16-18 13 unlike Moses, who put a veil over his face so that the children of Israel could not look steadily at the end of what was passing away. 14 But their minds were blinded. ... 16 Nevertheless when one turns to the Lord, the veil is taken away. 17 Now the Lord is the Spirit; and where the Spirit of the Lord is, there is liberty 18 But we all, **with unveiled face, beholding as in a mirror the glory of the Lord, are being transformed into the same image** from glory to glory, just as by the Spirit of the Lord. (NKJ)*

If the children of Israel looked up the mount or into the face of Moses (where God's fiery presence was reflected), they would have been transformed into the same image. **The key is, because they were *not* broken, <u>they did not want to change</u>.** (In a later chapter we will discuss the power of spiritual abortion regarding the destiny of God, and how God can redeem such a disabling place for a leader.)

When God reveals our destiny, He also is revealing what *moves* Him. God was moved by the cry of the children of Israel. Lost, oppressed and enslaved humanity is very close to

God's heart. He will reveal His most intimate secrets to a humble, *imperfect* man or woman, in order to set the captive free. In the same way people don't reveal their most intimate hurts and secrets to just anyone, neither does God. One of the reasons psychology is such a lucrative profession today is not because the masses are being emotionally healed. But rather, because people who are troubled do not want to reveal their innermost feelings to just anyone; they want to reveal them to someone who they believe they can trust and possibly can help. In the same way, God calls us by name and reveals His plan for our lives because He trusts that when we have come to a place of *brokenness*, we can be trusted with what is close to His heart. **A broken man or woman will always have a known destiny because he or she can be trusted with the intimacies of God's heart.**

5. **"He used and transformed Moses past."** The fifth and final aspect of this encounter with God, is that **God gives us the rod of His authority to carry out His purpose.**

> *Exod 4:1-5 1 Then Moses answered and said, "But suppose they will not believe me or listen to my voice; suppose they say, 'The LORD has not appeared to you.'" 2 So the LORD said to him, "What is that in your hand?" And he said, "A rod." 3 And He said, "Cast it on the ground." So he cast it on the ground, and it became a serpent; and Moses fled from it. 4 Then the LORD said to Moses, "Reach out your hand and take it by the tail" (and he reached out his hand and caught it, and it became a rod in his hand), 5 "that they may believe that the LORD God of their fathers, the God of Abraham, the God of Isaac, and the God of Jacob, has appeared to you." (NKJ)*

Here is a very powerful part of God's revelation of our identity and destiny. In addition to the process of Him calling us by name, changing the way we walk, humbling us by revealing Himself, and showing us His heart through Divine purpose, He also empowers us by transforming our life's experience into Divine authority. This doesn't mean that after we get to a certain age we can say to people, "Hey listen, I've been around for a while and I can tell you from MY experience..." That is a perversion of what God intended for us to learn from our life's adventures. It is not so we can lecture the young and condescend to the ignorant. Instead, what God intended for us to recognize was that through almost everything we have experienced in life (even back when we ran from the Pharaohs in our life), God was producing in us an sense of authority that (if necessary) we could part the Red Sea. For Moses, the summation of his life's experience came down to being a shepherd. He spent the latter forty years of his life tending the flock of his father-in-law. He defended them and fed them. He led them and even cared for them when they were sick. Now in Moses' moment of concern, when he questions, "God, What if?" God says, *"What is that in your hand?"* To put it another way, "What have you become?" Moses responds, "A rod (a shepherd of my father-in-law's flock)." God says, "Cast it down on the ground!" Again, to put it another way, "Cast down what you have become; you will no longer be a shepherd of your father-in-law's flock." According to the scripture, Moses flees with terror as the rod turns into a snake. (There is more to be revealed regarding this in the next chapter.) Then God speaks again telling Moses to pick up the serpent. When he does this, it turns back into a rod. From this point forward, the rod that he used to lead his father-in-law's flock, is no longer called just a rod. It is now called, *"The rod of God."*

Exod 4:20b *And Moses took the rod of God in his hand. (NKJ)*

Going back for a moment to a previous chapter in which we talked about demons obeying Paul and Jesus because they understood their identity, here lies the source of their unwavering authority. Many of us pray and shout commanding obstacles to be removed from our path. We pray boisterously for God to fulfill promises in His Word and bestow upon us the blessing we proclaim. We do this again on the basis of our legal right to proclaim what scripture says and the legal right to prayerfully use the name of Jesus. But when we get right down to it, many Christians live their lives with disappointment because of unanswered prayer and unresolved spiritual warfare. Why? Once again, the knowledge of our spiritual rights is necessary, but when the rubber meets the road, **knowing the technicalities of scripture and *having* an unwavering conviction that we can exercise those rights, is another story.**

When God told Moses to pick up the rod after he cast it down, God was saying, "Moses from this day on, you will be the shepherd of My flock, who are your people, and your forefathers' children." At this point, God demanded every thing that Moses had become. He had Moses cast that down before His presence, transformed it and returned it back to him, unveiling the hidden power within.

If the shepherd's rod was a symbol of Moses' vocation with his father-in-law, then we can safely say that the rod represented Moses himself. After all, the rod didn't make Moses a shepherd; Moses was the shepherd, the rod was just a tool. So when Moses picked up *the rod that God transformed,* in effect He was transformed and became himself, **"the Rod of God".** Another way of putting it is that **Moses, now transformed, saw himself as *God's instrument* and had the inner conviction and authority to call for anything he needed to fulfill his purpose.** This does not mean things went easily for Moses, but that he had a sense of dominion to forge his way forward. He could now stand in the face of any obstacle and fulfill his destiny. Why? Because his destiny was born from God's heart and he was now an instrument of it. It is this transforming discovery within each of us that says, "All that I have ever been and all that I have become, transformed by the hand of God, is for this purpose." **Moses was now transformed into a revolutionary.** He was ready to turn his world right side up, regardless how impossible it looked.

Men and women of God, God wants to transform all you are and all you have become into a conviction and *an authority* that can part seas of obstacles, make rocks gush with provision, and cause oppositions to bow to your decree.

When we have truly come to a place of *brokenness:*

- God calls us by name to settle us into our identity.

- He transforms the way we walk so we will remember who are forever.

- He reveals Himself so in humility, we can comprehend who we are.

- He opens His heart to us so we can see our destiny.

- He takes our past and transforms it into unwavering authority.

When we put this process together, in whichever way God may bring it about in each our lives, **God has created a *revolutionary* that can change the world.**

Chapter Eight
Revolution – Facing A New Tomorrow

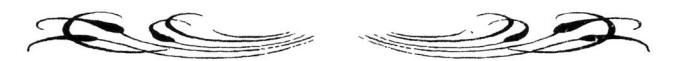

Exod 4:1-5 1 Then Moses answered and said, "But suppose they will not believe me or listen to my voice; suppose they say, 'The LORD has not appeared to you.'" 2 So the LORD said to him, "What is that in your hand?" And he said, "A rod." 3 And He said, "Cast it on the ground." So he cast it on the ground, and it became a serpent; and Moses fled from it. 4 Then the LORD said to Moses, "Reach out your hand and take it by the tail" (and he reached out his hand and caught it, and it became a rod in his hand), 5 "that they may believe that the LORD God of their fathers, the God of Abraham, the God of Isaac, and the God of Jacob, has appeared to you." (NKJ)

What an amazing feeling it must have been for Moses when he put his sandals back on, took his newly restored rod and set out for home with a clear sense of Divine purpose. Many of us covet the feeling that says with conviction, "My life has deep earnest meaning." "Nothing has been a waste." "All that I have been through, my birth, adoption, education, marriage, both good and bad, all the desert experiences, the times of refreshing, all crescendo to this point…**I am an instrument of the purposes of God."** *"I have been appointed to bring a revolution to the world I live in."*

This awareness is what produces a sense of dominion and authority in our lives. It gives us the ability to cross the deep seas of life and find a new shore on the other side. It gives us the ability to lead God's people with a steady confidence rather than a self-gratifying rightness. It causes us to look into the eyes of the Pharaohs of life and say, "Let 'My' people go!" It gives us such a command from within, that resistance from without is not in the equation. When Moses spoke those famous four words, he was not just speaking on God's behalf or rehearsing what God told him.

He was saying that these are MY people, for God's heart *is* my heart as well.

Rather than being encompassed with the passion to liberate the captive, it is evident that we, as Christians, fall into the trap of relishing our power over demons and over theology (Luke 10:17, John 5:39). When we see the lost and hurting as "our people" (as "our family"), the appalling reality that Satan may have them captive would enrage us like Pharaoh did Moses. It would not just result in picket signs and civil rallies, but powerful fervent prayer producing life changing results and sacrificial ministry. It would be that passion, which would go to whatever extent necessary to win the lost and liberate the captive. I remember when a certain female television personality "came out of the closet" on her television program, announcing to her audience and the world that she was a lesbian. I remember hearing the Christian community's outrage and many of them picketing the network that sponsored her. While I watched this happen, I realized I had a choice to either join the protest or not be a part of it. I was caught between what appeared to be right and what appeared to be apathy. When I confronted the Lord on this, He opened my heart and took me beyond my point of view. He said, "The reason My people protest, is because they haven't learned to pray with My passion." He pointed out to me that the tax collectors and the prostitutes are the ones who He ate with. The only ones He protested, were the religious people who saw themselves more righteous than the sinners (Matt 23:13, Luke 18:11-14). I realized then that my place was to pray for that young woman and those like her until they were free. I realized that it was my place to find a way to reveal God's love to them by my actions and by my words. Since then, our church has begun to experience ministry and growth to those who would have never set foot in a church that picketed and protested. The exciting thing is that the newcomers' conviction is not coming from me preaching against sin, but by them experiencing the presence of God's Spirit through the lives of loving people in the congregation.

When Moses came to the point where God's heart became his heart, that interchange formed a conviction that spoke with strength and authority. As we stated in the previous chapter, it was the transformation of the shepherd's rod that established the authority of God in the life of Moses. It was when God took all that Moses had become in life and transformed it into the instrument of God's heart, which gave Moses the unwavering ability to confront Pharaoh and lead God's people.

Picture this. Moses is standing in front of the burning bush and He is holding his shepherd's rod (which he used for forty years). Now he questions whether or not he would be received as God's man for the mission. So God says to cast this very familiar and life-long emblem to the ground. When Moses does this, the rod turns into a venomous snake. Moses quickly flees and is then commanded by God to pick it up by the tail. When he does, the snake is transformed into *the rod of God.*

We know from scripture, that the Israelites hated snakes and to them, they represented uncleanness, evil and wrongdoing (see Nelson's Bible Dictionary). Through this God was revealing that any sin, wrongdoing, mistake or negative experience in life can be transformed into something of value. Unfortunately when God confronts the ugly parts of our lives, revealing that they need to be transformed, we run like Moses. Approaching the pain in our past is not an easy thing to do. In spite of the fact that we may acknowledge that God is with us and He is leading us to do so, we avoid direct confrontation. Not only is the past scary to face, but our resulting lifestyle as well. The reality that what we have become, as Christians, may be questionable (our conduct, relationships and attitude), is even more frightening. The comprehension that our attitude toward people in the congregation may be self-centered and that our witness to the world may be self-righteous is hard to face. Preferably, we spend a lot of time reading books, attending pastoral counseling and joining prayer lines to be free from our problem issues. Though all these aspects are tools that God uses in our lives to aid and assist us in healing, only one element can ultimately free us from our past. That aspect is to cast our hearts before Jesus *in the valley of brokenness* and allow Him to transform our past into something meaningful. We spend a lot of energy trying to separate ourselves from the past, but God wants to transform it so we can be whole. If we attempt to disconnect ourselves from the past, whether good or bad, we will be incomplete as people. God desires to mend our hearts so we can return to our world with the same kind of conviction and authority Moses had. This is not to say that God commissioned negative things to happen in our lives so we could have meaning, but that in contrast to the fact that evil has happened in our lives, God would transform those experiences into valuable significance. It is in this sense of meaning, that we find an inner conviction and a confident strength for the future. It is not that we simply throw our past away and say we are free, but that the past, when touched by God, becomes the foundation of the future. When we recognize this, our future takes on a genuine sense of destiny and the past becomes a foundation for meaning. When you think of this process, keep in mind that the serpent Moses fled from at the burning bush, became a symbol of powerful healing later on in his ministry (Num 21:8-9). Think of Jesus now in heavenly glory. If you were to walk up to Him, you would still see the nail scars in His hands. **The fact is, what Jesus suffered in the past gives value to His ability to minister to us in the present.**

Heb 4:15 For we have not an high priest which cannot be touched with the feeling of our infirmities; but was in all points tempted like as we are, yet without sin. (KJV)

We, as Christians, have to recognize the place of our deep need to a point of brokenness, so we can touch the needs of others. We don't have to have the same exact kind of experiences, but if we understand where we have hurt, we will know how to reach the place where others hurt. If we do not, then we are nothing more than Pharisees disconnected from those who need ministry. There are many today in high places of ministry who have lost touch with the people they are ministering to. Recently a friend told me of a preacher whom while speaking to a church said, "I have always flown first class, and I will continue to fly first class," and then took up an offering for himself. That is a sure symptom of a paradigm challenge and the struggle to stay disconnected from its reality. Unfortunately, many people are moved by such types of Pharisaical statements and in the end, "covet" to be first classers, rather than "lowly" coach flyers. Yes, God wants to bless us; He doesn't care if we fly first class or coach or even own the airplane. What concerns Him is whether or not the suffering of those we minister to touches us. This is not a pious pity for those less fortunate than ourselves, but rather, a compassion that understands where the hurt abides. How? Because in some way we have been where they are. *Until we know the place of our pain and the comfort of Jesus, we cannot focus in on the pain of others and be an instrument of His hand.*

Another aspect of this experience is that the snake was not just some ugly past experience or spiritual condition, but it was also one of the highest ruling symbols in Egypt. **For Moses this was more than just a poisonous past; it represented the greatest power and deadliest authority in the world.** Let's think back for a moment and see what Moses' real problem was. Several chapters ago we found that Moses ran in fear from conflict, particularly from Pharaoh and from the Hebrew, who said, "Who made you ruler over us?" This about sums up all the conflicts of his entire future ministry. Because of that fact, God had to deal with the center of Moses issues. The most debilitating poison Moses had within him was his own fear. The transformation of the rod was the transformation of Moses central fears. This same fear of the serpent is what also kept the children of Israel in bondage to Pharaoh. They could not see themselves more powerful than he was. As a reminder the scripture said:

Exod 1:9 And he said to his people, "Look, the people of the children of Israel are more and mightier than we; (NKJ)

Pharaoh knew full well the potential of the children of Israel, but through affliction he kept their ability to overcome at bay. For Moses to transform the resignation of the oppressed from Pharaoh to Jehovah, he had to have made the transition from one to the other, as well.

Next, God tells Moses to take the serpent by the tail. This had to be even more frightening than the sight of the creature. Bad enough his rod turned into the serpent; now God is saying to pick it up in such a way that he could be drastically hurt...or even killed! (As a side note, being a one-time owner of non-poisonous snakes, the last thing you ever do is seize a snake by the tail. Poisonous or not, it can give you a painful bite.) The only way you can grab a poisonous snake by the tail is if you have someone else grab it by the head. Now think of this. If the snake represented Moses past, it was most likely a venomous cobra, which was the key symbol on Pharaoh's crown. God was making a strong point to Moses. Not only was He saying that He had taken "the whole of Moses' life" and transformed it into a meaningful confidence, **but He was also saying that through his newly found inner conviction, it would give birth to an authority that could take the highest known power (Pharaoh) by the tail and *without* fear command its course.** *The other subtlety God was saying was, "Moses, when the miracles start to happen and people start to follow, remember who has this project by the head so that it doesn't bite you."*

God is revealing to us that when we come to the place of brokenness, in meekness we are surrendering our most debilitating fears. When He confronts us to grasp those fears, there is a feeling of exposed vulnerability. In contrast, He is saying that the destiny and confidence He has laid before us, has an omnipotent power at the other end that will be available when we need it. Lastly, He is reminding us that when results start to happen we need to remember who is empowering our lives. We need to recall this moment, never forgetting the nail scars of our own lives and that it was through the scars that we have a valid message.

As God prepares Moses to return in Divine purpose to the children of Israel, God re-enforces His transforming authority.

> *Exod 4:6-9* 6 *Furthermore the LORD said to him, "Now put your hand in your bosom." And he put his hand in his bosom, and when he took it out, behold, his hand was leprous, like snow. 7 And He said, "Put your hand in your bosom again." So he put his hand in his bosom again, and drew it out of his bosom, and behold, it was restored like his other flesh. 8 "Then it will be, if they do not believe you, nor heed the message of the first sign, that they may believe the message of the latter sign. 9 "And it shall be, if they do not believe even these two signs, or listen to your voice, that you shall take water from the river and pour it on the dry land. And the water which you take from the river will become blood on the dry land." (NKJ)*

Here again God takes what was a very frightening disease, (leprosy) and makes His point. By placing Moses hand into his "bosom" (the place of his heart) and turning it leprous, God reveals the condition of Moses' life. By showing Moses his condition, he is able to validate his message for the children of Israel. According to medical diagnosis, leprosy (in addition to ulceration of the epidermis) yields loss of sensation, paralysis, gangrene (death and decay of body tissue), and deformation of limbs. God tells Moses in so many words, "Herein is the message that will set the children of Israel free." In effect the message of Moses was, "Oppressed of Pharaoh, I know your condition. I was even worse off than you. I lived in Pharaoh's house and lost the *sensation* of who I was. I was taught the ways of the serpent and was *paralyzed* in fear by its power. When I ran in fear from Pharaoh, realizing my own identity and destiny, I was slowly *decaying* in the desert. I lived a life of *deformed* compromise as a shepherd of sheep, rather than the shepherd of God's people." He would go on to say in afterthought, "You have lost the *sensation* of who you are. You have been *paralyzed* by your fear of Pharaoh. You have been *decaying* in oppressed slavery and you have been living a life *deformed* from your Divine destiny. But I have been sent by God to show you the way out." According to the scripture he was then told to take water from the Nile River and pour it on the land.

When he did this it would turn into blood. The Egyptians defined the Nile River as the god *Hapi*. *Hapi* was the god of provision and prosperity. Again the message of Moses' life as it related to his oppressed people went something like this: "I was born by Hebrew parents. But because of the power of Pharaoh, I was sent down the River Nile and placed into his hands. As long as I subjugated myself to Pharaoh I was used for his profit. I was going to be a ruler of Egypt and would have never known the God of my true fathers. But God had to pour out my life in the desert so I could become the man I was meant to be and the child of my forefathers. God had to draw my life out from being under the spell of the gods of Pharaoh and pour me out. I had to be emptied so I could be filled with who I am in God and accomplish His purpose." In similar fashion the conclusion of this message was, "You, too, have been used for the profit of the taskmaster and he has used your lack of identity for his own prosperity. Your fear of him has kept you in his clutches, but I know a way out. I know, as one more enslaved with his ideas than you, that there is freedom. If you will pour out who you are in the desert of brokenness and longing, God will give your life powerful, new meaning. You will once again be the sons and daughters of your forefathers and be the *revolutionary* nation you were destined to be."

> ***Exod 4:30-31*** *30 And Aaron spoke all the words which the LORD had spoken to Moses. Then he did the signs in the sight of the people. 31 So the people believed; and when they heard that the LORD had visited the children of Israel and that He had looked on their affliction, then they bowed their heads and worshiped. (NKJ)*

As believers, many times we think that theological study improves our knowledge of God. But in actuality, the scripture says that knowledge puffs up, but it is compassion that truly ministers (1 Cor 8:1; 13:14). Simply stating scripture is insufficient to have a message that will change the lives of others. The idea that picket signs which say, "Jesus loves you" can change the world is selling the power of God short. **We need to become the sign; we need to become the message.** You may say, "No kidding." But until we are poured out in the valley of *brokenness* and *transformed* by God's **compassion,** we have nothing but theological correctness. You may say that you know those who blare scripture and seem to have fruitful results, but remember, so did Pharaoh's magicians. They, too, were able to duplicate some of the things Moses did with the *Rod of God*, but in the long term their deeds were not born of God's compassion. They remained in the grip of Pharaoh's power. Later the scripture tells us that those who heard the message of Moses were not only the children of Israel, but also some from other nations, and of course, that included Egypt. In short, the magicians could have been freed as well, but they chose bondage instead.

In the life of Jesus the same happened with the Pharisees. The power of the Lord was present to heal them, but they chose their own blindness rather than who they were really intended to be.

Luke 5:17 *Now it happened on a certain day, as He was teaching, that there were Pharisees and teachers of the law sitting by, who had come out of every town of Galilee, Judea, and Jerusalem. And the power of the Lord was present to heal them. (NKJ)*

The difference between living in religiosity or *revolution* is living a life poured out for the purposes of God. Recently I was ministering a message at our church and a member of the congregation came to me and shared that she felt she needed to repent of "pride" and "fear." She continued saying that God showed her that **we, as a people, need to be free from the Pharisees that live within us.** How accurate she is! The Pharisee is one who subtly thinks of himself more righteous than another, then validates his posture with the legalities of scripture. He finds that his point of view is the correct one and the only one that is truly valid in his heart. The magician, on the other hand, is the individual who ministers to others because it is the spiritual thing to do. He calls upon the power of the Spirit, because down deep he wants to be spiritual like other Christians. Like the Pharisee, who is more concerned with winning a theological argument than having compassion on the hurting, the magician is more concerned with winning the spiritual battle rather than transforming the enslaved. Think of all the times that we, in the church, may have condemned the sinner by condemning his sin. We have been taught over the years to love the sinner and hate the sin; but we need to realize that what makes a sinner a sinner, is his sin. When we hate the sin, many times the message becomes confused and the sinner believes we are angry and critical of him or her. When Jesus was confronted by the Pharisees regarding the woman caught in adultery, he said to her, "Woman has anyone condemned you?" He then said (see John 8:11), *"Neither do I condemn you, go and sin no more."* Jesus made it clear that the person was more important than the sin itself. *His message to the woman was not focused on her sin, but her need for a Savior. It was about her wellbeing and making it clear that the Savior loved her more than her sin legally condemned her.*

All of us need to beware of the subtle Pharisees and crafty magicians that try to take residence within us. Let's not fall into the snare of trying to identify those around us who seem to be infected with religiosity or revival revelry. Instead let us identify our own condition. God is seeking to produce true *revolutionaries;* He is seeking to produce a people, who through earnest individual *brokenness* keep themselves purged from the Pharisees and magicians within.

I recently heard a story that went something like this: "There was a small village in a foreign country that had many needs. They would pray and ask God for answers all the time. In His faithfulness He would always answer them and provide what they needed. One day, a young man came into their village seeking sanctuary. He told them that there were military officers looking for him for a crime he did not commit. The people took him in and took care of him. Shortly thereafter the officers came to the small village inquiring of the young man. The officers threatened the people saying that if they did not produce the young fugitive, they would begin executing members of the village at sunrise. In fear, the people of the village went to their minister to ask counsel and prayer. Very troubled, the minister said that he did not have an answer, but would seek the Lord for one. He toiled all night and just before sunrise, he found the scripture that says, 'It is better for one to die, than a whole nation.' At dawn, the minister told the officers where the young man was hiding. They immediately took the fugitive to execute him. After the military officers left the village, the small village erupted into celebration. They made a large feast because the threat and danger was over. Unfortunately the minister did not partake in their festivities. Very grieved about the death of the young man, he retired to his room. That night an angel of the Lord appeared to him and said, "What have you done?" The minister replied, "I saved the village from a lethal threat." The angel replied, "How could you have done this thing! The young man that was seeking sanctuary was an answer to one of the village's most dire prayers." The minister replied, "How could I have known?" The angel said, "If you would have just put down your bible for a moment, gone to the young man and looked into his eyes, you would have known."

Stop for a moment, close your eyes and seek the presence of the Holy Spirit. Maybe at this point God has stirred in you a greater need for Himself. Maybe He has brought conviction to your heart and you sense that He would like to transform some area within you that has been left in darkness. Maybe you recognize that God wants to take the good Word that has been sown into your heart and make it a living expression in your life. Maybe you recognize that God has been at work in your life to bring you to a burning bush experience. Maybe now is the time to recognize that God has had you in a process to bring you to a place where in brokenness, you can be touched with the compassion of Jesus and begin (or revitalize) a life of purpose and ministry. Maybe God has shown you something else of value regarding your life that needs to be addressed. Stop for a moment. Put down this book and pour out your heart to the God who loves you.

Chapter Nine
Revolution – Abortion and Rebirth

2 Sam 6:2 And David arose and went with all the people who were with him from Baale Judah to bring up from there the ark of God, whose name is called by the Name, the LORD of Hosts, who dwells between the cherubim. (NKJ)

Of all the *revolutionaries* in scripture, the life of King David probably tells the story of success, struggle, holiness and sin like none other. It would seem that when we look at the broad scope of David's life, nothing really worked out easily for him. It would appear that there was conflict and opposition to his divine call since the days of his youth, until his last breath. Yet to this turbulent life, God Himself promised that the Messiah would reign over his kingdom and that his throne would be everlasting (Isaiah 9:6-7).

If David had a high school yearbook, his friends would have probably written, "Really cute musician with a future in his father's sheep business." In other words, no one would have guessed David's future. When God commissioned the prophet Samuel to seek a new king to replace Saul, Jesse (David's father), did not acknowledge David until after all of his "other" sons were presented to the prophet. When the giant Goliath threatened Israel and David arrived on the scene to help, he was reviled by his brothers. After the victory over Goliath, King Saul granted David favor and gave him the hand of his daughter, Michal. But eventually Saul became one of David's worse nightmares chasing him all over the land with the threat of death. For the most part, struggle never ceased for David, whether it was the death of his covenant brother, Jonathan, the rape of his daughter, Tamar, or the insurrection of his son, Absalom, every blessing came with contention. But in spite of all the challenges, David brought a *revolution* to his nation and for that matter the spiritual world, which has had an eternal impact on every soul throughout generations for both Jew and Gentile.

One of the pivotal moments of this *revolutionary* process was when King David brought the Ark of the Covenant back into his city. David wanted nothing more than for his people to be encompassed with the blessings and presence of God. Yet, with all his good intention things did not work out the way he had hoped. For David personally, this attempt toward *spiritual revolution* ended in trauma and sin. To put it another way, the *seed of revolution* he possessed, ended in abortion until God redeemed the matter.

After having spoken to ministers from different sized ministries and different parts of the world, I believe that many are like David. They have carried *the seed of revolution* in them and for some reason the process of bringing forth the revolution ended in devastation, much like a miscarriage or even an abortion.

SECTION ONE:
GOD IS DOING A "NEW THING" THROUGH AN "OLD PROCESS"

The trials started early in the project when the revival and excitement of its *revolutionary potential* ended in tragedy. The scripture says:

> *2 Sam 6:3-10 3 So they set the ark of God on a new cart, and brought it out of the house of Abinadab, which was on the hill; and Uzzah and Ahio, the sons of Abinadab, drove the new cart. 4 And they brought it out of the house of Abinadab, which was on the hill, accompanying the ark of God; and Ahio went before the ark. 5 Then David and all the house of Israel played music before the LORD on all kinds of instruments of fir wood, on harps, on stringed instruments, on tambourines, on sistrums, and on cymbals. 6 And when they came to Nachon's threshing floor, Uzzah put out his hand to the ark of God and took hold of it, for the oxen stumbled. 7 Then the anger of the LORD was aroused*

against Uzzah, and God struck him there for his error; and he died there by the ark of God. 8 And David became angry because of the LORD'S outbreak against Uzzah; and he called the name of the place Perez Uzzah to this day. 9 David was afraid of the LORD that day; and he said, "How can the ark of the LORD come to me?" 10 So David would not move the ark of the LORD with him into the City of David; but David took it aside into the house of Obed-Edom the Gittite. (NKJ)

The first issue that produced symptoms of stress was the placing of the Ark in the "new cart." It is interesting to note that the Hebrew word for "new" (chadash), is a wonderful positive word in most any other scenario. It means, "a new thing, to rebuild or repair." But here, when it comes to bringing a *spiritual revolution,* **the "new thing" is the cause of fatality.** You may ask, "But I have heard all over the land that God is doing a 'new thing,' He is 'restoring' and 'rebuilding' His church." I agree! The problem is that "new" does not necessarily mean "different." The "new cart" may have been state of the art. It may have been the latest and greatest thing since the "double oxen harness," but that did not mean it was the way God desired to bring *spiritual revolution* into the land. God seems only to have two ways that bring *spiritual revolution* and both are required. The first is a **paradigm change** (changing our point of view by *compassion)* and the second, is the **transforming process of brokenness.** The fact that we have the newest message, the newest worship song, the newest church growth philosophy or the newest evangelistic program, does not mean this is the vehicle God will use to bring *spiritual revolution.* In the American and European culture we have conditioned ourselves with the idea that if it is not "different" from the last "thing", it could not be *new and inspired.* The great danger of this pursuit of the "new/different thing" is that many times we abandon the process that God uses to bring *spiritual revolution;* the subsequent result is error.

In the case of "the new cart" and it being the vehicle that would bring the presence of God (the Ark) into the city, we find that it was the direct cause of major problems. As the scripture states, the Ark began to topple and Uzzah (which means, "strength", in Hebrew) puts forth his hand to keep it from falling.

The result is that Uzzah is struck dead which sends tremendous fear throughout the procession. *You will find that many of the "new" movements in the church are, in the long run, more of a hindrance than productive.* The reality was that the "new cart" could not sustain the Ark for the entire journey. The problem arose when the new cart with the Ark arrived at Nachon's Threshing Floor. Here is the first major key. The word Nachon in the Hebrew means, "prepared." **God has a process of preparation for *spiritual revolution* that <u>cannot</u> be changed** (regardless of how new or avant-garde we become in spiritual things). **Every *spiritual revolution* and *revolutionary* must be brought through a place of preparation producing *compassion* and *brokenness*.** When God began the process of bringing David and his men through the time of preparation (Nachon's Threshing Floor), that is when the Ark began to topple. The bottom-line is that <u>**the focus of**</u> the "new/different thing" doesn't have the ability to sustain the presence of God for the forthcoming *spiritual revolution*. As we stated in previous chapters, God will bring us through the desert to Mount Horeb (the place of desolation) or in this case, Nachon's Threshing Floor. *His purpose for bringing us to such places is not to discourage us, but to bring us to a point where **no other motivation exists within our heart** except His heart, His identity, His destiny and His compassion.* The fact that the Ark started to topple, was a direct result of the reality that the "new/different thing" could not proceed past the process of preparation. **To put it another way, the toppling of the "new" cart was actually *part of the process*.** Think of it this way, even at this point, if David had the Ark carried correctly, the procession still would have had to go through the rough terrain of Nachon's Threshing Floor. In other words, regardless of what our style of worship or theological bias, the process doesn't change. We still have to go through a time of brokenness with a discovery of compassion to bring *revolution*. You may ask, "What if we have the correct focus during the time of preparation?" Though our "focus" maybe correct, which may give us an understanding of what is happening (thus make it easier to go through the process);

it still doesn't mean that we will go through the process any faster. God is going to do things His way and take whatever preparations He needs to do it, for the benefit of the believer and His Kingdom.

By this event God begins to reveal the state of affairs. As the process continues, Uzzah put his hand out to stop the Ark from falling and was killed. When you think this through, the Ark just came from Abinadab's house because the Philistines previously possessed it. During that time, the Ark caused the Philistines all kinds of distress. In particular, when it was placed with the statue of the Philistine god, Dagon, the Ark caused the statue to topple several times and eventually broke it.

In short, David and his people experienced a revival. They were moved by God to desire His presence and they reached out to receive it. But during this revival, we find that Uzzah actually believed that **his strength was required** in the time of crisis. How many times do we, as Christians, convince ourselves that our strength is necessary to do what only God can perform? How many times in each of our lives have we sought God for change and at the first sign of Him moving, we jump right in and try to assist the process. The result of our assistance (rather than obedience) is what usually stops the progress, forcing us, at some point, to start over to some measure. Remember Abraham and Sarah? They are classic examples of this kind of behavior. God tells Abraham and Sarah that they are going to have a child. Rather than obeying God, they try to assist God by Sarah giving Abraham her servant Hagar to produce the child. The result was trial after trial [and their actions still impact the world (in particular the Middle East) today]. Eventually God had to deal with Abraham and Sarah to bring them to a place of brokenness so Isaac could be born. Jesus said in the Sermon on the Mount:

Matt 5:3 Blessed are the poor in spirit, for theirs is the kingdom of heaven. (NKJ)

The idea of being poor in spirit is the awakening that we have been talking about. It is the recognition of coming to a place of brokenness within our hearts; it is not limited to just needing a Savior. When we are poor in spirit, we can then encompass the Kingdom of Heaven within us (Luke 17:21).

The real puzzling part for me was why the Ark toppled. Why not the new cart break and the glory of God appear in the Ark? Or, why not an Angel of Lord appear and rebuke Uzzah and Ahio? Or, why not a prophet prophesy what needs to be done? Ultimately, it is not about the cart itself, supernatural manifestations, nor a man and his message; it is about the presence of God in and among mankind. After all, that is the Gospel message in a nutshell. The whole essence of the coming of Jesus was to be our Emmanuel (God with us). God is not looking for the "new," but *"the genuine."* To put it another way, we have a tendency to get spiritually bored, so we look for the "new/different thing," losing sight of God's transforming process.

Sometimes what God intends in the "new" and "different," is not what we assume or intend. Many times the "new" and "different" starts with the Holy Spirit, but ends as an action born of rebellious children who believe they need to leave what has *fathered them* to gain some sense of their own identity. Yet what the Holy Spirit intends, is that we discover the Father's purpose in the "new thing" and **its connection to Divine History.** As a reminder from the last chapter, it is similar to when Moses saw the "new thing" (the burning bush); this is where God first spoke to Moses connecting Moses to Himself, *the God of his fathers.* Thus, the new thing is supposed to be a catalyst propelling us forward to a place of maturity, so we can produce the *next spiritual revolution and generation.* Unfortunately what has happened in our religiosity (regardless of an individual's age), is that *the movement becomes the identity* and an avenue to find recognition among our spiritual or ministerial peers. This is much like what teenagers experience with they rebel against their parents for the sake of the peer group (or gang). But again, God is looking for the genuine. He is looking for men and women who not only recognize that they are children fathered by the previous generation, but He is looking for men and women who have come to a point of child-likeness (in humility); and men and women who are ready to build the future on the foundations of their forefathers. This doesn't mean that all traditions are acceptable or that previous methods applicable. But God is looking for the state of being within one's heart which can reproduce the same brokenness, compassion and humility in its children. He is looking for the genuineness of *His heart* in the individual, not the newness of the method or manifestation.

If I was David, and unaware of what we have just discussed, I would have said, "Hey God! What's wrong? We have the newest cart. We are playing the latest worship songs. We are wearing our latest Christian tee shirts... Lord, why has this thing happened? Uzzah was a man in your service and he sincerely believed that all we were doing was in Your will!" But God's response was clearly saying something else. He was saying, "The only way I am going to enter your city bringing *spiritual revolution,* is if you go beyond revival and *experience revolution within yourselves."* **God was exposing that the *assistance of man* was unacceptable, but the *brokenness of man* was mandatory.**

The first step in preparation was that the assistance of man's strength was to be removed. Unfortunately, David did not get the picture. Instead he was afraid. For many believers today this is where we are. Down deep on the inside we are disappointed that the vision God gave us has not completely manifested or in some cases we're afraid it never will. We may even secretly feel that God has misled us, but because of our religiosity, we do not admit such things to ourselves. It is hard to admit to ourselves that we are angry and afraid, especially of God. All we know is that a few years ago, things were better; God was moving, but now it is dry and difficult. For some of us in Word of Faith circles, we think that if we cast down our fears, hold on, keep professing the vision, it will come to pass. But in reality, **until we take our hands off of God's revolution, the revival journey will continue to topple and frustrate us.** If we were in some charismatic circles, after Uzzah died we would have rebuked the devil, attempted to call life back into Uzzah and tried to continue the journey. If we were in more of a traditional setting, we would have looked up to Heaven and said, "It must have been Uzzah's time; isn't it wonderful that he passed in the service of the Lord." All of these answers may have a spiritual resonance, but none of them truly reveal the state of affairs. When we, as Christians, (and sometimes ministers are the worst offenders) collide with the attempt of God to bring us to a point where our paradigm has to change and our lives have to be broken before Him, we tend to respond with such statements or actions. These kinds of statements are born out of two things: First, *"theological bias"*, which means that we only see situations from one spiritual bent, proving our lack of paradigm transformation, and obstinately act in the name of Jesus. The other is *"theological extenuation"*, which means that we really do not have a clue as to what is going on so we create some spiritual sounding answer to alleviate our sense of uncertainty.

David's response to the death of Uzzah was shortsighted, but in effect, correct. In so many words David said, "Forget this. Something is unacceptable here; we're not going anywhere." He then left the Ark with Obededom. In his fear and frustration, at least David was smart enough to take his hands off of the Ark of God. Today a lot of us in the church are trying to make things work and use spiritual or programmatic techniques to help us, rather than the humility of the heart. We speak correction without the *compassion of Jesus* and we grow our ministries by marketing techniques rather than the *humility of Jesus*. When we speak without compassion, according to scripture, we are false and when we solicit followers without humility, we are drawing them to ourselves. According to Jesus this is a Pharisee. Recently the

Lord opened my eyes to this analogy. **"There are only two kinds of Christians on earth: those who are anointed and minister and those who are anointed and minister *with brokenness.*"** Both have an anointing and both have results, but only one has the approval of God. After all Jesus did say:

Matt 7:21-23 21 *"Not everyone who says to Me, 'Lord, Lord,' shall enter the kingdom of heaven, but he who does the will of My Father in heaven. 22 "Many will say to Me in that day, 'Lord, Lord, have we not prophesied in Your name, cast out demons in Your name, and done many wonders in Your name?' 23 "And then I will declare to them, 'I never knew you; depart from Me, you who practice lawlessness!' (NKJ)*

To make the point even stronger, just because someone has a large following, a television program, an extensive tape catalogue, published books, a classy car, expensive clothing, an impressive title or a high position in the church, does not validate that one has come to a place of humility and brokenness. Only brokenness means brokenness, only humility means humility and only compassion means compassion. We, in the church, must recognize our state of affairs within our hearts. Sometimes we misuse our anointing or ministry success to prevent God's wooing to ward off brokenness. We misuse our success to blind our need for compassion and we misuse our relationships with "important people" to haze our need for humility. What's worse, is that our congregations are equally caught up in the ***illusion*** of what is approved of God. Jesus would have never warned, *"Many will say to Me in that day, Lord, Lord, have we not prophesied..."* if He had not foreseen that potent ministry would go on in the church and without being connected to His *revolutionary* eternal purposes. Once again we need to elevate the ministry of the Gospel to the high calling of God that it was intended to be, instead of a profession or worse yet, a boarding school fraternity.

2 Sam 6:12-15 12 *Now it was told King David, saying, "The LORD has blessed the house of Obed-Edom and all that belongs to him, because of the ark of God." So David went and brought up the ark of God from the house of Obed-Edom to the City of David with gladness. 13 And so it was, when those bearing the ark of the LORD had gone six paces, that he sacrificed oxen and fatted sheep. 14 Then David danced before the LORD with all his might; and David was wearing a linen ephod. 15 So David and all the house of Israel brought up the ark of the LORD with shouting and with the sound of the trumpet. (NKJ)*

(The fact that the house of Obed-Edom was blessed is very significant, but we will look at that at the end of this chapter.) After a time, David once again sets out to bring the Ark of the presence of the Lord into the city. But now a major change had taken place. David and his men were broken before the Lord and were now ready to bring *spiritual revolution*. You can see this by what David did and how his men proceeded. For one thing, God changed David's viewpoint and brought him to a place where status and position were no longer his focus of identity. Now he is willing to not only bring the Ark with great triumph and pomp, but worship and humility. Rather than using the latest and greatest, they humbled themselves and carried the Ark as proscribed in scripture (Num 7:9). The "new" cart had its purpose and brought them to the time of preparation (Nachon's Threshing Floor). But when they got there, the "new" cart could go no further. Only on the shoulders of humility could they go through the process of preparation for *citywide spiritual revolution*. To put it another way, the "new thing" is designed to bring you to preparation, but when the time of preparation begins, only *brokenness* and *compassion* will allow you to move forward.

Because newness appears to work within one city or church, doesn't mean it will work within another. You may find the reason it worked in one place, is because God's people allowed their hearts to be humbled and broken before Him. The "new thing" was the agent to bring compassion and brokenness to that city or church. On the other hand, you may find that God is leading a part of His people to brokenness by using some other means, like tradition. Whatever the case may be, we must allow God to be God and we must offer Him the genuineness of our hearts in honesty and worship. He is "seeking for such to worship Him" (John 4:23-24).

God is pursuing those men and women who desire to be *transformed* into whom He has ordained for them to be, rather than being *transmuted* into the latest style of worship or fad of message. You may say, "But John! When I went to that church (or meeting) I experienced such a powerful move of the Lord; I want our church to experience that." Great! But what do you want your church to experience? The same thing you did somewhere else, or what God desires to manifest for the vision and purpose He intends for your church. Years ago, I can remember several services where God's Spirit fell on us and we all broke into laughter and rejoicing. It was so refreshing. (This was before the days it was popular for an outbreak of laughter in a church.) I guess if I wrote a book on the Spirit of Laughter, televised those services and promoted them as something special, we could have started a "new thing" in the land. There were also times where the anointing for healing would come and as God would touch ailing people, legs grew out, backs were healed, and so on. There were also seasons where prophetic ministry would be the emphasis; God would move and the people would be encouraged. So many times we wanted to camp out and just stay in those services. Many times, those visiting in the services would say, "This is it! This is the church I was looking for." But as soon as God would sovereignty move us by His Spirit into other areas such as, faithfulness, accountability, humility, brokenness or serving with compassion, then those same people would leave. We have had many people who graced the doors of our church, received a touch from Jesus and then left when it came to becoming a *revolutionary* for Christ. Where would you find them? In the next church or meeting where God was refreshing His people, until He began addressing revolutionary issues again.

SECTION TWO:
THE SEED OF REVOLUTION ABORTED

All that we have discussed so far can be conceived as types of normality in the process of coming to and going through Nachon's Threshing Floor, the burning bush at Mount Horeb, or our time of preparation in identity, compassion, brokenness and destiny. The key point of a revolution being aborted occurs in the next segment of scripture. When David arrived in the city with the Ark of God, the bible tells us that his wife, Michal, was watching from the palace window.

> *2 Sam 6:16-23 16 Now as the ark of the LORD came into the City of David, Michal, Saul's daughter, looked through a window and saw King David leaping and whirling before the LORD; and she despised him in her heart. 17 So they brought the ark of the LORD, and set it in its place in the midst of the tabernacle that David had erected for it. Then David offered burnt offerings and peace offerings before the LORD. 18 And when David had finished offering burnt offerings and peace offerings, he blessed the people in the name of the LORD of hosts. 19 Then he distributed among all the people, among the whole multitude of Israel, both the women and the men, to everyone a loaf of bread, a piece of meat, and a cake of raisins. So all the people departed, everyone to his house. 20 Then David returned to bless his household. And Michal the daughter of Saul came out to meet David, and said, "How glorious was the king of Israel today, uncovering himself today in the eyes of the maids of his servants, as one of the base fellows shamelessly uncovers himself!" 21 So David said to Michal, "It was before the LORD, who chose me instead of your father and all his house, to appoint me ruler over the people of the LORD, over Israel. Therefore I will play music before the LORD. 22 "And I will be even more undignified than this, and will be humble in my own sight. But as for the maidservants of whom you have spoken, by them I will be held in honor." 23 Therefore Michal the daughter of Saul had no children to the day of her death. (NKJ)*

The scripture said that Michal, David's wife, despised him in her heart. By the word "despise," the Hebrew describes the idea of disesteem. The reason Michal did this was because she **did not** have a change in her point of view. She did not have a problem with the revival idea (which was to obtain and experience the presence of the Lord), but when it came to bringing a *spiritual revolution* to the city (through genuine ministry to the people), she could not comprehend it. She came from the perspective that the king should behave in a certain manner and to behave in any other way was unacceptable. She sarcastically accused David of dishonoring his position (verse 20). The key to her accusation was that **he lowered himself** to the place of the people. She said, *"...as one of the base fellows shamelessly uncovers himself!"* The

Hebrew language is very revealing concerning this statement. Another way to look at this scripture would be to translate it, *"...as one who bares himself as empty and poured out."* The word in Hebrew used for "shamelessly" did not mean acting immodest, but referred to an *empty vessel* or *a vessel that has been poured out.* What Michal was seeing as disgraceful, was actually what God had accomplished by taking David through Nachon's Threshing Floor; **God wanted a man who was willing to reveal that he was poured out before the Lord.** David was willing to take the power of his God-ordained position and in humility bring it to the level of the people. Only after the process of brokenness with humility was he able to bring the presence of the Lord (the Ark of God) into the city. Taking this a step further, only after he humbled himself and was poured out, was he granted the ability to truly bless each person in the city (verse 19) and return home with a genuine blessing as well (verse 20).

David did not waste any time contemplating Michal's disdain; he immediately addressed her point of view. He said, *"And I will be even more undignified than this, and will be humble in my own sight."* There was much to this contention between Michal and David. He retorted stating that God chose him in lieu of her father. Here is an important comparison: Michal saw the world *through the eyes of Saul* and **compared David to that image.** *She saw the Kingship as something above the people and separated from the people.* Today many in various ministry positions have this perception and even worse, **many congregations (like Michal) perpetuate this illusion.** The simplest forms of such an *illusion* is why people get offended with the minister when he makes a mistake or a poor decision. As a minister friend of mine once put it, "Did you ever notice that people want others to act more like Jesus then they do? And then they get offended when others don't!" This is why sometimes people who seem to have status in the church carry more of a voice of authority and influence than the pastor and eldership. This is why many times people in congregations are comparing ministers to ministers, ministries to ministries, or what they have seen happen in one place to what they see in their own circles of fellowship. We, in the church, need to break free of the *illusion* that Michal lived in. Why? Because the results of such illusions are bareness and sin (verse 23). The *illusion* that ministry is acceptable without brokenness and humility in the life of an individual, is nothing more than a *mirage.* It's bad enough that many of us preachers went into ministry without any kind of brokenness, fueled by our own illusions of grandeur. Worse yet, our congregations and followings help shape the deception from which we minister. Members of the congregation help perpetuate this *illusion* when they compare one minister to another, one ministry to another, one elder to another, and so on. The individual Christian must come to a place where he or she can be submitted to their pastor, their eldership and inter-related with their fellow-members **without** comparison. If not, when brokenness occurs in the life of the leadership, we will stand at our window of observation judging and criticizing what we see, even though we do not understand what has happened. In the end, we will become barren to the things of God.

David, having gone through the process of *brokenness* and enlarged in his perception through compassion, was not only willing to be undignified, but desired to maintain humility in his own eyes. **He was willing to worship and minister to the people from the viewpoint of his own emptiness.** Like we said in the previous chapter: *"Until we know the place of our pain and the comfort of Jesus, we cannot focus in on the pain of others and be an instrument of His hand."* David could now bless the people of the city because he was emptied of himself and now filled with the blessing of God. Though he was anointed as king a long time ago, his ministry took true validity when he became an anointed king who was poured out before the Lord *and the people.* So rather than being separated from the people, he took his position of authority and in compassionate humility he touched the people. The humility he acquired by going through the time of preparation empowered David's kingship to make a difference throughout the city and the nation. This is what God wanted. But because Michal still lived in and refused to change her state of perception, *the revolution was aborted* and for David the end result was sin.

The scripture points us to a very powerful statement in the following verse, *"Therefore Michal the daughter of Saul had no children to the day of her death."* Up until this point, God did not say who would be David's heir. By natural law, it was usually the firstborn, which would be Amnon, but Amnon was born prior to David's kingship and not of royal blood. By royal blood, Michal, the daughter of the former king (and rightful queen of Israel) was the wife through whom the heir should have been born. This blessing that David brought home was clearly connected to whether or not Michal, would have children, thus David's heir to the throne. When she at this point rejected David, thus her own brokenness, the blessing was withdrawn from her and she never gave birth to the intended heir. For David, this must have been a tremendous point of distress. The idea of coming home after such a personal experience of transformation, carrying the blessing of *spiritual revolution* and future destiny, only to be scorned by his wife must have been devastating. The scripture in the following chapter (2 Sam 7) tells us that David desired to build the Lord a sanctuary. Shortly thereafter, it says that God spoke to the prophet Nathan and revealed to David that it would be David's heir who would build it. In the subsequent chapters, the bible reveals that David was victorious in war, extended continual blessings to the people and ruled with righteousness. But for David, personally, he had no wife to bear the heir of his throne and construct the sanctuary he longed to build. *In other words, David had a blessing given to him by the Lord with no way to see it realized.* Because of this overwhelming realty, the scripture says that David could not sleep and one night walked out on his roof.

2 Sam 11:1-2 1 It happened in the spring of the year, at the time when kings go out to battle, that David sent Joab and his servants with him, and all Israel; and they destroyed the people of Ammon and besieged Rabbah. But David remained at Jerusalem.

> *2 Then it happened one evening that David arose from his bed and walked on the roof of the king's house. And from the roof he saw a woman bathing, and the woman was very beautiful to behold. (NKJ)*

We all know the rest of the story. David saw Bathsheba, had her brought to him, slept with her and she became pregnant. Upon finding out she was with child, David had her husband, Uriah, brought from the battlefield with the hope that he would sleep with her and no one would know what happened. But Uriah was loyal to the king and fellow soldiers and would not engage in pleasures while they were at war. To save face, David had Uriah assigned to the most dangerous part of the conflict, with the hope that Uriah would be killed; and of course, he was. On top of all that when the child was born of Bathsheba, it also died. For David, one who had such a revolutionary experience, he probably never could have felt so low as he did then.

The blessing born of *spiritual revolution* that God intended for David and Michal (which was to produce the potential heir to the throne), ended in disgrace, sin and tragedy. David had the seed of future revolution for the next generation within him, but with no womb to plant it. This frustration led to disillusionment, sleepless nights, neglect of what he was supposed to be doing (a time when kings went to war), and eventually sin.

I know of several ministers who struggle like David. God brought them through a time of brokenness and planted in them the *seed of revolution*. But because those around the leader did not receive the same transformation of paradigm, they could not see what their leader was seeing. *The result was barrenness where the future was to be born.* This frustration can produce all kinds of problems, if not immorality, some other form of detached disappointment. Many Christian leaders have fallen into some type of sin or some kind of detached discouragement because of inappropriate, or a *"no"* response from those who were to assist them with bringing the revolution to the next level. **Do not be fooled into thinking that it is all the leader's responsibility to** produce a *spiritual revolution* and win a community of people to Christ. **IT TAKES BOTH LEADER AND CONGREGATION TO BRING THE PRESENCE OF GOD TO A CITY AND ESTABLISH A LIVING SANCTUARY.** If God brings a leader through a time of *brokenness* (birthing the *seed of revolution* in his or her heart) and if the congregation **refuses** to respond appropriately, there will be barrenness.

I experienced this personally. Years ago Karen and I were commissioned by God to leave our temporary residence in Texas (where I attended and graduated from bible college) and return to California. When we arrived in California, the Lord spoke to my heart and said that we were to go to the church we attended several years prior to us moving to Texas. Two days before we attended our first Sunday service the Spirit of the Lord spoke to me again and said, "I have called you to pastor that church." I was excited and scared at the same time. The Sunday we arrived at service we could plainly see the church was in trouble. When we left for Texas some two years earlier, the church was thriving with anywhere from 75 to 125 people in any given service. Now there were only about 12 people in the entire sanctuary including a few young children. As we sat there we listened to the pastor speak. At the conclusion of the message he said in so many words, "I have not shared with any of you what I am about to say except with the eldership. Today is my last service as pastor of the church; I am leaving having resigned my position." I almost fell out of the pew! I remember shaking as the senior elder took the pulpit and said, "God told me he will be bringing a young man to pastor the church." I went from shaking to feeling overwhelmed. I knew that I was that young man. Throughout the next week I shared the vision God had given Karen and me along with the passion to take the city for Christ. However, by the end of the week the leadership felt that I was not the young man for the job. I was devastated! I felt that I had moved 1,500 miles with the word of the Lord in my heart for a church and a city, now all for nothing. I cannot describe what it felt like to have experienced such rejection, but if you have been in a similar situation, you know how deep the pain can go. For nine months I could not think. But eventually God began a process of redemption, bringing me back to the vision and the ability to pursue it.

The key point to this story is that well over a decade has passed and the church that rejected the man with the *seed of revolution* went through four different pastors and is still barren in its influence in the city. I believe the time has come for those who have rejected revolutionary moves of God in the past to repent. I believe we are in a time where God will open an opportunity for people and congregations to be restored to their place of revolution and give birth to destiny.

For the person with the *seed of revolution* in their heart who has experienced such trauma, if they do not obtain the wisdom of God on how to respond to the negative matter, they will find themselves like David, in trouble. Some have sought to gratify their grief with lusts and self-indulgent sins. Others detach themselves from the joy they once had in ministry and subtly erode into a passive faith and maintenance ministry. In such situations, you hear the unaware in the congregation say things like, "I knew that what brother (or sister) so and so claimed would never come to pass. See him (or her) now. The fire is gone; I knew that it would not last." Or, "What a shame. That man (or woman) of God used to preach and teach so well, but now they have fallen into sin and will never minister like that again." With such statements, the individuals who utter them never realize that God will hold them accountable for what happened in the life of their leadership.

Ps 106:32 *They angered Him also at the waters of strife, so that it went ill with Moses on account of them... (NKJ)*

Moses, a man that was broken before the Lord and ministered for years with a strong anointing, ended his ministry without seeing the fulfillment of his destiny. The reason for this unhappy ending was because Moses messed up and aborted the mission (See all of Numbers chapter 20). But even though God dealt harshly with Moses (and Aaron), the book of Psalms tells us that things went badly for them *because of the children of Israel.* The result was that an entire generation would stay in the wilderness and die before God would move the next leader, Joshua, to take the land. For David, the rejection of Michal, all that he went through with her earlier in their marriage, left him ill-fated. The result of unfulfilled passion (much like in our example in chapter 3 with Samson) rarely ends with an appropriate action.

Maybe you are that minister in whom God did something wonderful and when you brought your *revolutionary passion* to your board, congregation, or leadership, it appeared to fall on deaf ears. Maybe you are that minister who left that moment of rejection, discouraged and with a feeling of disconnection from your future. Maybe you have the feeling that what God has born in you will never come to full maturity, because those who you thought would stand with you, didn't. Maybe you resolved your unfulfilled passion for the impossible, with settling for ministry life that is existent in *"dependable mediocrity."* Stop right there and do not allow your "theological bias" or "theological extenuation" to rationalize this away. No! God did do something powerful in you and what he put in you he will bring forth! You may say, "But John, I have fallen into serious sin; there is no way I can go back and minister." Wrong! If David can "in genuineness," repent for a season, get back up, and move forward, so can you! As a matter of fact, God will take the very calamity your are in and *transform* it into the vessel through which *revolution* will come.

We know it is biblically sound to say that any man, woman, or group of people, who have fallen into sin, can be restored. But we must remember that *restoration* in the New Testament by virtue of the word is very different than *restoration* in the Old Testament. In the Old Testament Hebrew, "restore" predominately appeared as two different words. The first is, "shalam" which means: to repay.

*Joel 2:25 "So I will **restore** to you the years that the swarming locust has eaten, the crawling locust, the consuming locust, and the chewing locust, my great army which I sent among you. (NKJ)*

The other word, is "shuwb" which means: to return, to go back or bring back.

*Ps 23:3 He **restoreth** my soul: he leadeth me in the paths of righteousness for his name's sake. (KJV)*

Both of these Hebrew words suggest two different types of restoration, but neither of them actually addresses the issue at hand. The fact that God brought forth Solomon through David and Bathsheba reveals that restoration doesn't always mean to return or go back, which is the Old Testament definition of "restoration" from the concept of "shuwb." In this case "shuwb," would not only require David to return back to Michal and produce the heir, but for Michal to return to David with a change of heart. This is not what happened; for that matter what God did was to take the worst of the situations and He brought the New Testament type of restoration which is even father reaching.

Gal 6:1 Brethren, if a man is overtaken in any trespass, you who are spiritual restore such a one in a spirit of gentleness, considering yourself lest you also be tempted. (NKJ)

The Greek New Testament word for *restoration* is "katartizo." This word describes exactly what happened in David's life; it means: to complete thoroughly, to mend and to put in order.

Until David fasted and wept for the child born of adultery (2 Sam 12:21-25), David's house had the pending judgement of calamity according to the prophetic word of Nathan. But once the child passed away and David accepted the consequences of his actions, God gave the couple a new start and a new child, Solomon. Not only did they receive such a new start, but God also called upon the same prophet (Nathan), to give the baby a spiritual name, Jedidiah, Beloved of God. The end result of the restoration was completeness and a return to the order in which God intended things to flow. In this case it was not an issue of returning back to what was, but for God to complete David's destiny. It was for God to mend the pain of both David and Bathsheba's sin and return to order the original state of things by bringing forth Solomon who was the Beloved of God and the "heir" of King David.

If you are man or woman of God who may have experienced a revolutionary abortion and then found yourself painfully grieving in the arms of sin's comfort, know this. If you will stay poured out before God, transparent before those you are accountable to and broken before God's people, your greatest days in the presence of the Lord are ahead of you!

In the saga of David and Bathsheba, David made some serious mistakes; he committed adultery and covered his sin through murder. But God once again breaks all the natural rules and brings forth life from death. He takes this union between David and Bathsheba and produces through them a second child, the heir to the throne. Through David and Bathsheba, God brought forth Solomon Jedidiah, whose kingship brought his nation to levels of international recognition that surpassed his father's reign and built a magnificent sanctuary which fulfilled his father's vision.

SECTION THREE:
THE REBIRTH OF REVOLUTION

This now brings us to what may appear to be the most challenging element of all: how a congregation, denomination or fellowship of people who realize they may have contributed to the abortion of a *spiritual revolution* come to rebirth. Such a people may ask, "How can we return to the place of pregnancy once again and birth what God desires among us?" Of course the hardest step is realizing that one participated in such an abortion because self-righteousness never leans toward repentance, but self-justification. If church history has taught us anything, we must agree that time and time again, God has had to go outside of the organized church and find someone who would obey Him to the point of revolutionary fullness. As we mentioned in the first chapter of this book, men and women of God, like Martin Luther, John Wesley, Aimee Semple McPhearson and so on, all had to leave the organized church to revolutionize their world. But this is clearly not God's best or first choice. The scripture never suggests this as a norm and for that matter, God desires a unity (John 17) that will convince and convict the world to faith in Christ. As long as we keep splintering to revolutionize, we weaken our God ordained potential.

So how does a congregation come back to revolutionary birth? The answer lies with the Ark's temporary abode in the house of Obededom the Gittite. According to the scripture, while the Ark was at Obededom's house, he was very blessed because of the presence of the Lord. For three months the Ark of the presence of the Lord stayed there. But that was enough for a young man name Ittai (a relative of Obededom) to experience a rebirth of *spiritual revolution* in his life. He came to a place in his experience with God where nothing mattered. He just wanted to be where the presence of God was. He was willing to go wherever and with whosoever, as long as the presence of the Lord was there.

2 Sam 15:19-22 19 Then the king said to Ittai the Gittite, "Why are you also going with us? Return and remain with the king. For you are a foreigner and also an exile from your own place. 20 "In fact, you came only yesterday. Should I make you wander up and down with us today, since I go I know not where? Return, and take your brethren back. Mercy and truth be with you." 21 And Ittai answered the king and said, "As the LORD lives, and as my lord the king lives, surely in whatever place my lord the king shall be, whether in death or life, even there also your servant will be." 22 So David said to Ittai, "Go, and cross over." Then Ittai the Gittite and all his men and all the little ones who were with him crossed over. (NKJ)

David's comment, *"Why are you also going with us? Return... For you are a foreigner and also an exile..."* is a real powerful statement. There is a statement of rejection, a clear statement of not belonging and being banished or exiled as a person. All these statements are pointing toward the disconnection of destiny and purpose. There are congregations, maybe even denominations that are solely being held together by virtue of their inability to break the barriers of their paradigm and rediscover *brokenness*. The inability to rediscover the presence of God exists, because as a body of people we keep trying to place the presence of God into the very frame that caused us to abandon it. It is no different than when a group of leaders from an assembly get together to discuss the need for change without having anyone in the group experiencing the change needed to lead the way. The result is, they simply take the same equipment they already have and reposition it. It looks somewhat different at first glance, but the results are the same. When a church changes leadership and doesn't experience transformation, then the problem is not necessarily the leadership, but the congregation themselves. Why? Because they may have changed leaders, only to select someone who sees things they way they do and thus perpetuate the bareness. Some denominations as a rule change pastors every two years. While the rationalization is good, if the congregation doesn't experience a rebirth of *compassion, brokenness* and *destiny,* they will only maintain their function in the community, rather than transform it to revolutionary proportions. So you may say, "Dr. John, how can I find the burning bush (mount Horeb) again? How can I find the place of preparation (Nachon's Threshing Floor) and pass through again?" Ittai's reply has the powerful substance we as a people and congregation need, *"As the Lord lives, and my lord the king lives, surely in whatever place my lord the king shall be, whether in death or life, even there also your servant will be."* Ittai recognized this; David had the Ark and wherever the Ark was, the presence of the Lord was. Ittai found his rebirth of vision in the presence of the Lord and by submitting to leadership that had experienced the same brokenness. He was a foreigner, but not to the presence of the Lord. He was an exile, but not in the acceptance of the Lord. He was rejected, but not in the purposes of God. The humility of Ittai born in *brokenness*, which he discovered as a rejected, disconnected and banished man, is what gave him a new purpose. The only way congregations can experience such change is when they come to a place where nothing else matters but the tangible presence of God in their corporate life. One of the earmarks of such a transformation is not just in a spiritual or philosophical change, but change in a very practical sense. It occurs when the congregation is willing to join with leadership to follow God and experience Him regardless what the cost. It's as the old song says, "Where you lead, I will follow." This is not to blindly follow some charismatic personality, or spiritual manifestations, but follow leadership who have been broken by the presence of the Lord and ministers with *compassion* before the people.

*2 Sam 18:2 Then David sent out one third of the people under the hand of Joab, one third under the hand of Abishai the son of Zeruiah, Joab's brother, **and one third under the hand of Ittai the Gittite**. And the king said to the people, "I also will surely go out with you myself." (NKJ)*

Ittai became one of the top three commanders in the *revolution* David brought back to his land. Ittai (a banished man for sins unknown to us), was given the highest command in David's military. **Ittai is the congregational example of revolutionary rebirth.** Ittai found a humility that said in so many words, "The true approval of God is on David and the presence of the Lord goes with him. I don't care what position I hold or what I am asked to do; all I know and care about is to be with the presence of the Lord. All I care about is to be with a leader who has been poured out in brokenness and has the approval of God on him." Ittai knew that David was a man of *compassion, brokenness, humility* but also an **imperfect man.** For Ittai, David was a man approved of God. Ittai did not live with a religious *illusion* of what position and status brings. He lived with a clear understanding of what he was without the presence of God and wanted nothing more but to serve the Lord with leadership who understood the same. When a congregation is brave enough to admit their sins to God and their leadership, not just in moral aspects, but in how they relate to and follow leadership, then pregnancy can begin once again.

Joshua experienced this same rebirth with the children of Israel after spending 40 years in the wilderness. They said:

Josh 1:16-17 *16 And they answered Joshua, saying, "All that you command us we will do, and wherever you send us we will go. 17 "Just as we heeded Moses in all things, so we will heed you. Only the LORD your God be with you, as He was with Moses. (NKJ)*

This is what it took to take Jericho, Ai, and the five kings that fought against Gibeon. The same is what is necessary to take our cities and our nations. It is not just an anointed service with spiritual manifestations, but an anointed *broken* people, who follow *broken* leadership with the *compassion* and authority of Jesus. Now we transform ourselves from "doing" church, to being the church, which is the house of the presence of the Lord.

Chapter Ten
Revolution – Transcendent Love

> ***Rom 8:35-39** 35 Who shall separate us from the love of Christ? Shall tribulation, or distress, or persecution, or famine, or nakedness, or peril, or sword? 36 As it is written: "For Your sake we are killed all day long; we are accounted as sheep for the slaughter." 37 Yet in all these things we are more than conquerors through Him who loved us. 38 For I am persuaded that neither death nor life, nor angels nor principalities nor powers, nor things present nor things to come, 39 nor height nor depth, nor any other created thing, shall be able to separate us from the love of God which is in Christ Jesus our Lord. (NKJ)*

Several chapters ago we began to explore the key that transformed Moses from the viewpoint of living life as an Egyptian to a discovery of his God appointed identity and destiny. We found that the key was the supernatural power of the *compassion of God*. **It was this *compassion* that took Moses from looking at the world through the eyes of his own mind and allowed him to go beyond the barriers of it.** When we approach God from the standpoint of theological correctness or spiritual manifestations, we will be limited by the finiteness of our way of looking at the world. Consequently, when we minister to those around us, many times unbeknown to us we spend more time trying to maneuver people over to our idea of who and what God is, rather than introducing them to God, Himself. In addition, even though we are aware that we "don't know everything," and have limitations in our understanding, we are *unaware* of our boundaries. Unlike a walled yard, where the boundaries are clearly marked by brick and cement, our worldview is more like a sphere. In the walled yard scenario, if we are walking from one end of the yard to the other, we will eventually run into the opposite wall and recognize (even if we don't understand what a wall is) that for some reason we are being hindered. It would be like handing an average fourth grader the scientific formula of "Special Relativity" by Einstein and asking him or her to explain its components. Most likely the child will look at the symbols on the paper and then look up saying that they don't understand. But when it comes to the "sphere" scenario, it is as if we start walking in one direction (toward what seems to be a new and ever changing horizon), only to find that after we have expended our efforts, exhausting all the ground ahead of us, we are once again standing in the same place from which we started. The danger of religiosity is that we assume we understand based on the current status of information we have and we actually believe we can draw a conclusion with some accuracy. This would be like handing a scientist the formula of "Special Relativity" and leaving out a few key elements to the equation, then asking the scientist to use only the information given to arrive at Einstein's solution. If the scientist approached the challenge like many of us do in our spiritual life, he will assume the information he has is all the information he needs. Then regardless of how man times he manipulates the formula, if he arrives at the same solution more than once, disregarding that it differs from Einstein's, he believes that his must be correct (or worse yet, assumes he has arrived at Einstein's answer without checking). So like with the Pharisees and magicians that can potentially live within us, most of the time we don't recognize that the perspective we have will only lead us to the same shortsighted conclusions over and over. This is why religiosity is so repulsive to the world. The people in the world recognize to a point that they are in some kind of prison, so they acquire addictions, illicit life styles, false religions and so on, to alleviate the trauma of feeling trapped. In that light, when a Christian is bound by the powers of their own religiosity or corporate revival revelry, the world responds with objection. (This is not because the behavior or the viewpoint of the Christian is so divine that it reveals the world's need and in conviction they run. This, of course, is the illusion that many of us Christians have chosen to believe.) Though the world recognizes that the Christian **has something unique within,** they object to transferring from one prison to the next to obtain it. In short, it is as if we, in the church, have imprisoned the Gospel with the shroud of religiosity and/or revival revelry. Thus, the reaction of the world is hesitation and criticism. When the religiously infected believer sees this response from the world, he or she takes it as a need for spiritual warfare prayer, or a validation of his or her own spirituality, when in fact, it is a revelation of their own need for prayer to regain true spirituality and seek the affirmation of the Heart of God.

Several years ago, when I was struggling with my own walk with God, I remember one night listening to some classical music. Without any previous signal, the Holy Spirit spoke to my heart and said, "John, stop trying to be a perfect Christian and become a whole one." I realized then that I was trying so hard to fit a self-constructed religious mold which came from a viewpoint of what successful Christianity was, that I was constantly battling the power of discouragement, sin, and guilt. Yet, every time I would minister the Gospel, the sense of God's presence, anointing and affirmation would encourage me. The result was a host of mountaintop and valley (roller coaster type) spiritual experiences. But being a whole person, as it states in the scripture when Jesus cleansed the lepers, is quite different than just being healed of the disease alone.

Luke 17:14-19 14 And when he saw them, he said unto them, Go shew yourselves unto the priests. And it came to pass, that, as they went, they were cleansed. 15 And one of them, when he saw that he was healed, turned back, and with a loud voice glorified God, 16 And fell down on his face at his feet, giving him thanks: and he was a Samaritan. 17 And Jesus answering said, Were there not ten cleansed? but where are the nine? 18 There are not found that returned to give glory to God, save this stranger. 19 And he said unto him, Arise, go thy way: thy faith hath made thee whole. (KJV)

Here the active worship of the tenth leper is the result of recognizing the Jesus who loves him, is the one who touched him. The result of coming in contact with the *compassion of Jesus* changed this man from doing the religiously correct thing (which was to go to the Jewish priest) and instead, opened his eyes to *"see"* that the priest he needed to show himself to, was the one who healed him. By turning back and in gratitude worshiping God, the man was made whole. To make the point stronger, the nine who did not return were simply not whole. They were healed by God, but never saw or recognized the potential for *revolution*. Keep in mind, that in the previous verse (13), they did call upon Jesus, call Him Master and asked him to have mercy on them. Yet, even though they experienced such a wonderful cleansing from Jesus, they were not whole. Here again is the reality of experiencing revival and still being bound by and returning to Pharisaical life. In short, the nine lepers had a revival that died and the tenth had *revolutionary* change. The tenth leper could no longer in any manner return to his former way of life; he encountered the love of Jesus and "turned back," experiencing a *revolution*.

Once again, the "sphere" scenario has us looking in all directions but in whichever direction we go, we always come back to the limitation of where we started. To put this yet another way, my son has a set of building blocks that when stuck together make a car. Regardless of what he tries to do with those blocks, anything else is a deformed image of a car. When we take our spirituality from the standpoint of theological pursuits and/or charismatic manifestations of the Spirit, we are simply using the blocks that God has given us and creating a deformity of what He intended. What God intended for the church begins with a simple foundation...*His Holy Love*. **When with God's blocks we build something apart from His design, we may call it the *Love of God*, but it is a deformity of what the manufacturer intended.**

Now you may be thinking as I have that if we pursue theological correctness or utilize the spiritual manifestations that God has given us, it will result in revealing the *compassion of Jesus* to the world. But until we are **agents of that compassion within our own hearts,** we only reveal our lack of it. When we like Moses, Jacob, David, Peter and most all biblical heroes, come to a place of brokenness and allow **the *Love of God* to encompass**

us, we will be the agents of transforming revolutionary love that we were intended to be.

The Apostle Paul said:

> **Eph 1:18** *{I pray that} the eyes of your heart may be enlightened, so that you will know what is the hope of His calling, what are the riches of the glory of His inheritance in the saints, (NAS)*

Because we are limited by our own point of view, it is only through the revelation of Jesus (who is the manifestation of *the compassion of God)* that we can have the eyes of our heart enlightened. It is then through that realization, where we can discover our calling, live in our inheritance and minister with value to each other and to the world. The power of this revelation of *the compassion of God* reaches its highest declaration in the virgin birth, death, and resurrection of Jesus life. The challenge at hand is that the *Love of God* is a person and not just a story. The truth of God is a person, not just a story and for that matter, life everlasting is a person and not just a story. You may say, "I understand that; and God has commissioned us to preach that message to the world." True, but God did not tell us to tell a story or give an oration alone, but rather to become the story and the message ourselves. In the same way that the love, the truth and the eternal life of God was embodied in the person of Jesus, the Church is commissioned by Jesus, to also become agents of that love, that truth, and that eternal life of God. If when the message was first revealed, it was embodied in the person of Jesus, then we must conclude that the message was never intended to be imprisoned by symbols, styles of music, order of services, or even the lack thereof. The result of such things is a deformity of God's original intention. The reality is that the church was and is to become the habitation of God (Eph 2:20-22). When God inhabits us we then become an expression of the love and compassion of God. Another way of putting it is, to come in contact with the compassion of Jesus is come in contact with His presence. When we have encountered and have been transformed by the presence of the Love of Christ, then our study of scripture and yield to manifestations of spiritual gifts will produce a clearer expression and presence of what God intended for the world. Recently the Lord gave me this analogy:

- Ministry is people present with people.

- Worship is people present with God.

- The Kingdom is God present with His people.

- The Church is God through His people present in the world.

The idea of the presence of God being among us, touching our lives and through us touching others, is the *revolution* God seeks to occur in us and through us. The consistent revelation of the Love and Compassion of God is the center of experiencing and expressing God's presence. This is why the burning bush experience is so necessary in our lives. To come to a place of brokenness is the realization of all we lack in comparison to the person and presence of God. Then in accepting and yielding to the truth of His gracious love toward us, we discover who He has intended for us to be and we can then transcend all boundaries, previous viewpoints and limitations. The result is taking on the heavenly perspective that His compassion brings toward the world.

The idea of love transcending boundaries is nothing new to the human outcry. In many ways the power of love transcending boundaries has been written and expressed by mankind for ages. To give you a few examples, let's speak of parental love and romantic love. In our first example, a young man in the military will consistently write home to the family he loves. The power of their love toward him comforts him while he is behind enemy lines in the crossfire of war. A letter from his mother or wife provides the strength necessary to face the potential of death every day and grants him hope for the future. In addition to such letters, a small photo may be kept in his left breast pocket over his heart. The comfort and encouragement it brings him, almost assures him of obtaining impossible odds. The power of this love also transcends the borders of death. If you have never been in a real war, several movies in recent years have depicted war so graphically that many people have been deeply affected by them. In such films, that same young man who wrote home and received letters from home, keeping the picture of his family over his heart may unknowingly step on a land mine. After the initial blast and his body broken, in the last moments of consciousness, the young man will call out his mother's name for comfort or if possible, clutch the photo in his breast pocket, visualizing the family he loves so dearly as he approaches the point of his death. The point of this example is not to horrify us to the evils of war, but to point out the power of love and its expression. The love of a parent or spouse crosses enemy lines, empowers the recipient to perform impossible deeds against impossible odds, gives hope when no hope is in sight and grants comfort in the moment of death to face the eternal world to come.

In the same way, great writers and composers have moved audiences with the message of love and its power to transcend the boundaries of the mind. In 1595, William Shakespeare wrote the powerful play called, "Romeo and Juliet." Here the story unfolds when two young people fall in love despite their upbringing and social differences. Against all opposition, Romeo and Juliet seek to embrace the love within both of them almost blind to the social implications it is causing. In the final moments of the play, Romeo and Juliet surrender their lives to death, believing that in the next world their love would be possible. The thought that this literary work has existed for 400 years and still moves audiences to tears says something for its content. At the very least, the fact that this couple's love drew them to the point of death envisioning the peace beyond it almost virtually speaks of the Gospel.

John 3:16-17 16 "For God so loved the world that He gave His only begotten Son, that whoever believes in Him should not perish but have everlasting life. 17 "For

God did not send His Son into the world to condemn the world, but that the world through Him might be saved. (NKJ)

The power of the love and compassion of God crossed the boundaries of all opposition and empowers us to embrace a life that transcends the finite picture of death. For the Christian, there is no death; it is just a passage way to a greater life.

Richard Wagner's "Tristan und Isolde" (written in 1857), tells of two people drawn together by a love that would break all that was legally and morally correct. They would risk their own lives even to its end. Their bond of love was so powerful and knitting, that together they would resolve that their union would find its greatest peace in the world to come. In the final act of the story, Tristan (after receiving a mortal wound to his side) sustains himself until he knows Isolde is near. Upon hearing of her arrival, he rips the bandage from his side knowing that his death would be eminent. But knowing that Isolde's is near, her love would grant him the comfort and courage to face death and enter world to come. In her arms he breathes his last breath in hope. The power of their union not only grants Tristan courage to go into eternity, but His love and hope also draws Isolde to follow him there as well. With virtually a supernatural vision she sees her hero in the spirit world, longing to be with him. Knowing that in that world, their love would know no boundaries, she expires as well. Here again is another Gospel type statement in allegorical language. Jesus, contrary to what we legally and morally deserved as sinners, pursues us even to the death of the cross. In the subsequent hour of His death, He, too is wounded in His side from which blood and water flows. The All-Powerful Love of God enters the chambers of eternity clearing a path for His bride, the Church to join Him in eternal boundless celebration.

These stories of romantic love that have captivated audiences for hundreds of years should give the Christian church a clue for a need to go beyond revival and step in to a life of spiritual revolution. After all, God has revealed to us the greatest love that could ever be expressed in Jesus Christ. Even the pages of the precious Word of God that we read do not reveal the power of this transcendent love until it is made flesh in the life an imperfect human being reaching out to a lost world.

In the same fashion of the love tragedies told by the great writers and composers of the past, Hollywood, in recent years released a movie that impacted the nations much like Shakespeare's "Romeo," and Wagner's "Tristan." The name of that movie was, "Titanic." In addition to its Oscar awarding winning landslide and multi-millions made at the box office, a phenomenon occurred. Men and women of all ages returned to see this three-hour tragedy over and over again. Why? Was it because we all have a fascination with sinking ships and dying people? No! It was the love story that transcended the bounds of social status, and political correctness and gave overcoming strength, empowering the living to persist, transcend death and welcome eternal life. Once again it was an emotional experience with a retelling of a form of the Gospel. Sure is was not the truth of the Gospel in itself, and some may miss the point of the movie by getting wrapped up with a moment of immorally and riotous dancing between the couple, but like Jesus put it in Matthew 23:24, "We strain at gnats and swallow camels." What is amazing about Titanic is that it drew people to pay for a ticket each time to see it over and over, week after week. On top of that, those who went, told their friends and invited them to experience the movie as well. Think about it. Hollywood woke up one morning and said, "Hey everybody, we are all on a ship, destined for an iceberg. While most of the passengers will meet their death, a select few will survive. Among them will be a young woman who, through the power of love, will be changed forever and look forward to her last breath as an elderly woman so she can meet her lover in the world to come." If that is not an allegory of the Gospel, what is? The real issue is, whether it is Shakespeare, Wagner or Hollywood, they are only stories moving the masses. The reality is that you and I and the world, are all really on a ship called, "Earth," spiraling toward an iceberg called death. No one will escape it, but there will be survivors. The only ones who will survive are those who come in contact with people in the Church who minister the Gospel in a manner that transcends social and racial bias, what is politically correct, morally incorrect, and so on. It will be those believers, who will lead the passengers of the ship called, Earth, to the Savior Jesus. He will by His Spirit, empower them to change their lives forever, looking forward to the day they will see Him face to face when they transcend the power of death.

Several years ago I was struggling with some sin in my life that basically kept me guilty and faithless. As I cried out to God for help, the Holy Spirit opened my heart to this statement, "What got you saved, will keep you saved." What that meant to my heart was, "The righteousness of Christ granted to me by the compassion of God, is what got me saved, then that, and that alone is what will keep me saved." It was easy to focus in on how righteous Jesus was and is, but to allow the compassionate love of God to touch my guilty life was not easy. As a matter of fact, when you are "legalistically challenged" (that is the politically correct statement for being a self imposed Pharisee), it is easy to stay guilty in life, ineffective in the Church and nauseating to the world.

I am convinced that when each of us experience personal renewal and revival, if we seek the *seed of spiritual revolution* within it, we will move on into the intentions of God. If we allow God to develop that *seed of revolution* within us (which demands the brokenness we spoke of previously), I believe that the transcending compassionate love of Jesus will touch the world in ways the church has not yet seen. Rather than just going to see movies and stage works over and over and paying all kinds of money for tickets and videos, the world will come to experience the church, over and over, telling their friends of the clear tangible love of God in His people not on the big screen or the stage, but in real tangible life.

Matt 11:12 *"And from the days of John the Baptist until now the kingdom of heaven suffers violence, and the violent take it by force. (NKJ)*

REVOLUTION – "The Revolution was effected *before* the War commenced. The Revolution was in the minds and hearts of the people; a change in their religious sentiments of their duties and obligations. . . . This radical change in the principles, opinions, sentiments, and affections of the people, was the real ... Revolution."

- **John Adams** (1735–1826), U.S. president. Letter, 13 Feb. 1818.

A Special Thank You

I would like to take a moment to thank my wife and colleague in the ministry, *Karen,* who not only proofed this book several times (with my grammar that is no small task), but also put up with the long hours of not having me around while I labored to produce this work.

I would like to thank my friend, colleague, and bishop, *Dr. James O'Neal,* who through many conversations helped me stay focused and affirmed the inspiration of the ideas within the pages of this book.

I also would like to say a ***special thank you*** to *Marie, Judy, Julie, Big Tom, Jim, Father D'Maria and the rest of the crew* of *Domenico's Italian Restaurant* in Monrovia, who prayed for me, encouraged me, and many times allowed me to stay for long hours as I worked on my laptop writing; it was as if you gave the anointing on my life a place to flourish while you kept me fed with the best Italian food this side of Italy. *You guys are the best!*

I would like to thank *Jesus Is Lord Christian Center,* and in particular our *Pastors' Aids, Joni and Gloria* who prayed relentlessly for this book to be published.

And last but not all least I would like to thank the *Lord Jesus Christ* who is consistently merciful and gracious to me inspite of all the reasons I give Him do be otherwise. *To Him, be all the Glory!*